THE HALIFAX CITADEL

Brian Cuthbertson

Photography by Julian Beveridge

FORMAC PUBLISHING COMPANY LIMITED

HALIFAX 2001

Formac Publishing Company Limited acknowledges the support of the Cultural Affairs Section, Nova Scotia Department of Tourism and Culture. We acknowledge the financial support of the Government of Canada through the Book Publishing Industry Development Program (BPIDP) for our publishing activities.

Printed and bound in Canada

National Library of Canada Cataloguing in Publication Data

Cuthbertson, Brian, 1936-
The Halifax Citadel

Includes index.
ISBN 0-88780-517-5
1. Halifax Citadel (Halifax, N.S.)—History. 2. Halifax Citadel (Halifax, N.S.)—Guidebooks. 3. Fortification—Nova Scotia—Halifax—History. I. Beveridge, Julian II. Title
FC2314.H34C88 2001   971.6'225   C2001-900510-5
F1039.5.H17C88 2001

Formac Publishing Company Limited
5502 Atlantic Street
Halifax, Nova Scotia
B3H 1G4

Distributed in the United States by:
Seven Hills Book Distributors
49 Central Avenue
Cincinnati, OH 45202

CONTENTS

FOREWORD

The music of the pipes and drums, the thunder of marching feet, the crack of rifles — these are the sounds that greet visitors at the Halifax Citadel National Historic Site of Canada, and which invite them to experience life in a British garrison as it was over a century ago. Since 1980, Parks Canada has celebrated the Citadel's past through an exciting living history program. In 1993, they entered into a partnership with the Halifax Citadel Regimental Association (HCRA) whereby the association would manage this program and provide visitor services.

Since its inception, HCRA staff and volunteers have dedicated their efforts to building a world-class presentation and thereby creating a greater awareness of the Citadel's history. Men and women are recruited to re-enact the daily routines of two British army units that were stationed in Halifax at the Citadel between 1869 and 1871 — the 78th Highland Regiment and the 3rd Brigade Royal Artillery. The recruits are trained according to exacting standards laid out in infantry and artillery manuals used by the British army in that period. They wear uniforms that have been painstakingly assembled to original specifications. The dedication of the

recruits and the attention to detail that has been paid in bringing these two regiments to life is in evidence at the Citadel every day during the summer. Members of the 78th Highlanders remain active year round and have become a familiar sight at many ceremonies and events throughout Halifax. The reputation of the 78th Highlanders has also led to numerous appearances at festivals throughout Canada, as well as the United States and Britain.

Halifax was founded in the 18th century for military and political purposes. Its strategic importance was underscored in the 19th and 20th centuries and continues to the present day. Halifax is now a large metropolitan city that encompasses a container port, many universities, high-tech industry, as well as a military and naval base. For over 250 years civilian and military life in Halifax has revolved around the four successive forts. The HCRA is proud to work in partnership with Parks Canada toward protecting and presenting this important historical site. We trust that Brian Cuthbertson's book will inspire you to return to the Halifax Citadel again and again.

David Connolly
President, Halifax Citadel Regimental Association

Part 1

INTRODUCTION

Halifax Citadel is a 19th-century fort in the centre of the largest city in Atlantic Canada. The natural landscape of the area encompasses a magnificent harbour overlooked by a drumlin that rises more than 220 feet (75 metres) above sea level. On the eastern slope of this hill the first settlement and fortification were shaped by English settlers in 1749. The present star-shaped fort, whose walls are just visible above the green sward of Citadel Hill, is one of Canada's most visited National Historic Sites, attracting more than 130,000 visitors each year. It is one of the best surviving examples, in Canada, of a bastioned fort.

The steep climb from the city centre to the Citadel can be achieved by a set of stairs adjacent to the Town Clock. As part of the defence complex that developed when Halifax was one of the four principal naval stations in the British Empire in the 19th century, the fort offers a unique view of the geography and the history of Halifax Harbour. From the ramparts it is

Main entrance to Halifax Citadel

possible to pick out among the office towers and hotels, the historic military landmarks, such as Royal Artillery Park and the Naval Dockyard, that were at the hub of activity in this British outpost.

The first section of this book looks at the fort today — its historic buildings, the fortification and the displays of artifacts available for public viewing. The re-enactment of military exercises by men and women in authentic uniforms of the 78th Highlanders and the 3rd Brigade Royal Artillery is an important part of the activities in the Citadel. The 78th were stationed in Halifax from 1869 to 1871 — a time when many reforms were being introduced to soldiers' living conditions. This book looks at day-to-day life in the garrison and the regiment's participation in the town's social life, combining both contemporary photographs and the historical record to give a fascinating glimpse into the life of British soldiers on Canadian soil.

Chapter 1

TOUR OF HALIFAX CITADEL

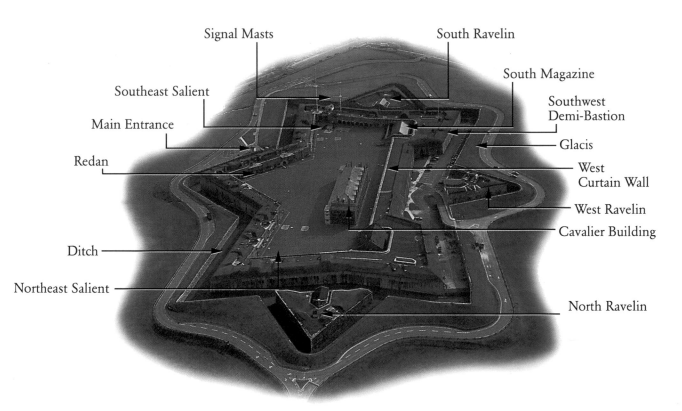

Signal Masts

South Ravelin

South Magazine

Southeast Salient

Southwest
Demi-Bastion

Main Entrance

Glacis

Redan

West
Curtain Wall

West Ravelin

Cavalier Building

Ditch

Northeast Salient

North Ravelin

The British military engineers who drew up the plans for the Citadel and oversaw its construction were steeped in the theory and practice of building forts laid down by Sebastien Le Prestre de Vauban, a 17th-century French military engineer. Construction of the present fort, the fourth to have been built on this hill, was begun in 1828 and took almost thirty years to complete. Its purpose was to protect the naval base that, in turn, protected the British colonies from American invasion. During the 1860s and 1870s the Citadel was of crucial importance to the defence of Halifax. By the 1880s, however, the evolution in armaments was making it obsolete and defence shifted to the harbour approaches.

It still served as the headquarters and barracks for the British Garrison until 1906, when Britain withdrew. The two-year period (1869-71) when the 78th Highlanders were garrisoned in Halifax is the focal point of Parks Canada's and the Halifax Citadel Regimental Association's presentation of the fort's history.

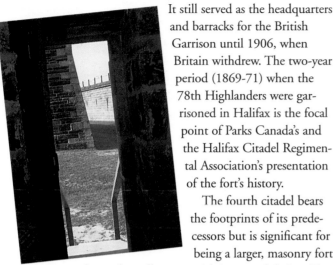

Entrance to the musket gallery

The fourth citadel bears the footprints of its predecessors but is significant for being a larger, masonry fort with improved design. To accommodate its size the crest of the hill had to be cut down several metres. The Parade is enclosed by stone walls and a ditch that are visible as one approaches the main entrance. The perimeter of the fort is extended and made less penetrable by the addition of the redan on the east side, and the three ravelins. The southeast and northeast salients are triangular, like the redan, while the demi-bastions on the southwest and northwest corners are portions of a four-sided bastion.

Attack was least expected on the eastern front, where the fort's main entrance is placed. When it was first built, entrance was gained by a drawbridge over the dry ditch (it

Guard on the bridge

The dry ditch with the curtain wall on the left.

was not a moat) that created a defensive barrier against attackers attempting to reach the walls and blast their way into the Citadel. Varying in width from 27 to 47 feet, the ditch, 20 feet deep, formed a crucial part of the defence perimeter.

In the high wall facing the ditch, technically called an escarp, there are openings through which 24-pounder cannon could fire at attackers as they tried to enter the ditch using ladders. Beside these fire ports are loopholes from which defenders could also fire muskets. Across from the

Guard Room

escarp is the counterscarp, a narrow cavernous gallery running the full perimeter, with just enough interior space for soldiers to fire and reload their muskets. They entered this gallery through sally ports in the Citadel's walls that lead

Snider-Enfield guns in the Guard Room

from the Parade, into the ditch and across to the counterscarp. From within the musketry gallery, defenders could fire on the enemy who would have had to face a murderous crossfire from both the musketry gallery and the escarp.

The 78th Highlanders

Sentries were posted day and night at the Citadel's entrance. Today, members of the Citadel's 78th Highlanders perform this duty. A ceremonial changing of the sentry is performed every hour. In or near the Guard Room, soldiers are available to explain their highland dress and be photographed.

Between 1869 and 1871 the 78th Highlanders was one of the two British Army infantry regiments in the Halifax garrison. When Parks Canada chose this regiment for its thematic interpretation of the Citadel, it was bringing to life memories of a well-loved regiment, at a time of peace and prosperity in Halifax. Each spring men and women are recruited for summer employment as guides and animators. They are trained in the 19th-century dress and drills of the 78th Highlanders and of the 3rd Brigade Royal Artillery, which manned the Citadel's guns.

Those of the Royal Artillery dress in blue serge with red stripes on their trousers and wear pill box hats. They are trained to fire the noon cannon located on the eastern ramparts above and to the right of the entrance. In the 19th century, garrison troops drilled daily on the parade square, which is divided into the main Parade, directly in front of the Cavalier Building, the North Parade and the South Parade. Today, the Citadel's 78th Highlanders perform daily, reenacting those drills. Both the 78th's pipes-and-drums and drill

Schoolmaster (right) and members of the 78th Highlanders re-enacting daily activities in the Parade

3rd Brigade Royal Artillery headdress

squads perform at national and international events.

Although British Army regulations restricted the number of wives to six percent of a regiment's strength, women were very much part of the regimental family. Wives and children lived in barracks and received free rations. Wives could supplement their soldier husbands' meagre pay by doing such chores as laundry and scrubbing out the privies. Regulations also required that all children up to 14 years old had to attend the Regimental School, presided over by the regiment's schoolmaster. Within the Citadel, in a casemate near the South Magazine, there is a schoolroom exhibit equipped with a

Soldiers' wives

magic lantern. A present-day regimental schoolmaster in his distinctive uniform of a cap, blue frock coat and black trousers, gives demonstrations of the magic lantern to the delight of visiting children. Soldiers' wives are portrayed as well by interpretative staff.

Cavalier Building

In the centre of the Parade is the Cavalier Building, first constructed in the 1830s and modified in the 1870s with a third storey. Like the rooms around the perimeter of the Parade, it is composed of vaulted chambers, called casemates, which are designed to withstand heavy bombardment. During a siege they were the safest places and could accommodate a full garrison of a thousand men. Most of the casemates served as barrack rooms or housed cannon to fire into the perimeter

The schoolmaster (left) gave instruction in basic literacy to soldiers and their children

Cavalier Building

South Magazine

Barrack room in the Cavalier Building

ditch. In the Cavalier Block, each of the first and second storeys had seven casemates designed to serve as barrack rooms for 10 to 12 soldiers. Originally the building had a flat roof on which cannon were mounted to fire out over the ramparts, but later these were removed because of the excessive weight on the structure.

Magazines

The most heavily protected buildings in the fort were those designed for gunpowder storage. Both the South Magazine and the South Expense Magazine are open for public viewing. The former, located at the southwest corner of the Parade, is a free-standing granite building protected by the ramparts. It could hold up to 2000 barrels of explosives in its cool, dark interior. The South Expense Magazine is accessible by a set of

Granite (left) and ironstone (above) walls need constant maintenance because of the effects of the harsh winter climate.

steps from the ramparts. The original North Magazine has been replaced by a red-brick building in the North Parade and the North Expense Magazine, not open to the public, is similar to its southern counterpart. On the ramparts there is also a mobile magazine, which, like the expense magazines, was designed to be used to hold cartridges for easy access on the ramparts.

Gun embrasure on the parapet

The Ramparts

After the invention of cannon and gunpowder, no masonry walls could withstand continuous bombardment. One form of defence was to excavate and build up the ground in front of the ditch. The excavated earth, created a steep slope — the glacis — which protected the walls from direct cannon fire. As further protection to the walls and ramparts — the Citadel's main line of defence — military engineers like Vauban added projections, giving the fort's perimeter the shape of a star. The Citadel's

Armament were mounted on the ramparts.

View of Citadel from Camp Hill

ironstone and granite walls formed the escarp and the retaining wall, between which were the ramparts proper made of packed earth, wide and firm enough to mount cannon weighing many tons. On the outer edge of the ramparts was the parapet, an embankment of piled sod designed to protect gun crews from enemy fire. Cannons were mounted at the v-shaped embrasures along the parapet.

Armament Against Sea and Land Attack

Against wooden warships, muzzle-loading, smooth-bore 32-pounder cannon were the most effective weapons in British service. When the Citadel was completed in the mid-1850s, the first guns mounted on the ramparts were smooth-bore 32-pounders. Mounting these, and later much heavier guns, was a major operation for which the broad ramp, located next to the South Magazine, was essential. The guns were placed on high-wheeled carriages and then 40 or 50 men hauled them up the ramp to the ramparts.

Guns were mounted on the ramparts behind the parapet

Such 32-pounder smooth-bore cannon were manned by Royal Artillery 10-man gun detachments. Today, the Citadel uses seven-man detachments for display purposes. Three men were used to get shot and cartridges for repeat firings, and are unnecessary for present-day needs. Smooth-bore cannon had an effective range of not more than 1500 yards. At that distance they could, it was calculated, hit a target 75 to 80 times out of 100 shots, with the crews firing one round every minute. At 2000

Land service mortar

At the northeast corner, formed by the east wall and that of northern front, there is one of a new class of rifled muzzle loaders, five of which were mounted in 1865 for the Citadel. These RMLs were of 9-inch (12 ton) and 7-inch (7 ton) types. They fired a solid-pointed projectile or a hollow explosive shell with projecting studs which could be rammed down from the muzzle end with the studs riding in the rifled or grooved barrel. On firing, the shell was propelled up the bore with the studs riding in the grooves, imparting spin. Rifled weapons had much greater range

Maintenance and repair of guns

yards a gunner's chances of hitting his target dropped to 45 percent.

The introduction of ironclads — wooden battleships protected by armour plating — was a revolutionary change. To deal with new naval capability in the 1860s and 1870s, muzzle-loading 32-pounders were converted from smooth-bore to rifled muzzle-loaders (RMLs), also known as 64-pounders. The word "rifle" derives from the German *rieflen,* meaning "to groove." Cannon along the eastern face overlooking the harbour are examples of converted smooth-bore 32-pounders.

Mobile magazine

and accuracy than smooth-bores, but above all they could penetrate ironclads.

Although these RMLs had a maximum range of 6,000 yards, gunners preferred to fire at 3,000 yards, ample in range and speed to penetrate an ironclad trying to pass the Citadel defences into Halifax's inner harbour. RMLs required a highly trained 9-man gun crew and took two and a half minutes to load and fire, compared to one minute for smooth-bore 32-pounders.

When the Citadel was being planned in the 1820s, landward attack was considered a major threat. The Citadel was most open to assault from the west, by a force landing on the shore of the North West Arm or in the area of St. Margaret's Bay. Invading troops would have sought to seize the hill some 700 yards to the southwest, today the site of Queen Elizabeth

Smooth-bore cannon cut away to show cartridge and cannon ball

II Health Sciences Centre and Camp Hill Cemetery. This would offer an invader a protected site for siege batteries and for massing troops for an assault. When British troops were preparing in 1758 to capture the great French fortress of Louisbourg on Cape Breton Island, they camped in rows of tents on this hill — hence its name.

For the western front, every effort was made to overcome the disadvantage inherent in the narrowness of Citadel Hill. Four-sided projections (technically named demi-bastions) were built at both the northwest and southwest corners. These bastions could cover each other's flanks with fire and sweep the ditch with cannon and musket shot. As with the north and south fronts,

a ravelin (a triangular fort separated from the Citadel proper by the perimeter ditch) provided added protection. On the west ravelin, with its fortified guard house, were mounted 32-pounders to give added protection to the long connecting wall of the west front. Its guns could also cover the glacis in front of the two demi-bastions. No cannon were mounted on the long wall connecting the demi-bastions, but on the Cavalier Building roof behind, seven 32-pounders were mounted *en barbette* — to fire over the western ramparts and out beyond the glacis.

In 1856, when the first weapons of the Citadel had been mounted, the western front boasted two massive, smooth-bore 8-inch shell guns, one in each corner, and 20 smooth-bore 32-pounders. Two decades later, such was the revolution in military technology, especially with the introduction of rifled armament, that all guns from the western front were dismounted. All emphasis now was on defending against steam-powered and heavily armed warships, which could bombard Halifax from greater and greater ranges. Only the eastern and southern fronts retained their guns. By the

Shells for the rifled muzzle loaders

Signal disk

1890s, no heavy armament remained as the outer forts took over the defence of Halifax against attack by increasingly powerful battleships and cruisers.

Signal System

As the command centre for a complex of smaller forts located on the approaches to Halifax Harbour and the North West Arm, the Citadel was the chief station for a visual signalling system. This system, located on the southeast salient, overlooking the harbour, consisted of two masts, which have been reconstructed as part of the Citadel's restoration. The military mast was part of a visual telegraph system, which first became operational in the 1790s, during the war with revolutionary France. By means of flags and balls, and at night by lanterns, messages could be sent between the Citadel and the outer forts.

As part of this system, a station at Sambro, at the outer sea approaches to Halifax, would report on whether

Commercial mast (left) shows the arrival of a Cunard steamship. The mast on the right was used for coded military messages.

incoming vessels were enemy or friend. If appropriate, a flag denoting this intelligence would be flown from the tall mast to alert naval and military forces. On the commercial mast would appear the flag denoting the vessel's origin; for example, blue stood for the West Indies. Below the Signal Station on the Parade are casemates housing the exhibit for the signal system used in the 18th and 19th centuries.

Firing the Noon Gun

For nearly a century and a half, a gun has been fired at noon from the Citadel every day of the year except Christmas Day. Whether a 32-pounder gun of the past or a 12-pounder signal gun was fired, the drills varied only in minor details and in the number of gun crew. For the firing of the noon gun, fewer crew are employed

Signals are hoisted on the mast daily, as they would have been in the 19th century

Signal cylinder

Soldier animators carry equipment to the ramparts for the daily firing of the noon gun

than would have been the case in real action. The Citadel crew, dressed in mid-19th century Royal Artillery uniforms go through the full drill, as used in the 19th century, for firing smooth-bore guns.

Within a gun crew, each soldier has certain tasks to perform and is designated by a number. For example, No. 1 commands and lays the gun on its target. No. 2 sponges out the bore and rams down the charge and the cannon ball. Another crew member, usually No. 5, fires the gun. Other crew lever the gun into position.

Before firing, a smooth-bore has to be cleared to remove with a wadhook any debris left by the previous firing. Next, a crew member

The gun is moved into position

(Above) Soldiers re-enact the drill with exactness
(Left) The sound of the noon gun carries over a large part of the city

inserts a wet sponge to extinguish any embers left in the bore so the next charge does not prematurely ignite. A rammer is used to push home the charge of black powder and after it, the cannon ball.

All this time the gun has been sitting on its carriage at the rear of its platform, well behind the parapet for the crew's protection. In the case of a 12-pounder, as few as two men can lever the gun forward into its firing position, but for a 32-pounder, which weighs as much as a small car, a full crew was necessary. A "preventor" rope acted as a brake. Once the gun is in position, No. 1 lays the gun on its target by line of sight, with the others using levers to elevate or lower the gun to adjust the range or move it right or left on his orders.

Before the gun can be fired, No. 7 inserts a priming iron

into the vent at the breech end to break the gunpowder charge. He then inserts in this vent a friction tube, containing a small explosive charge, and attaches a lanyard to a pin at the top of this tube. The lanyard acts as a trigger. On the order to fire, he pulls on the lanyard, drawing the pin from the friction tube, detonating and igniting the powder charge, which propels the cannon ball out of the gun's barrel. This drives the gun back into its original position behind the parapet so the firing sequence can begin again.

The Town Clock

Below the Citadel on the glacis is the Town Clock. In the 1790s, the commander at Halifax was Prince Edward, fourth son of George III and later, father of Queen Victoria. Edward was a firm believer in punctuality; the Town Clock was his inspiration. He had in mind a garrison clock, to be placed on the south slope. In the end, the military designed and constructed the tower for housing the clock, the local government provided the building over which the tower was built and it was erected on the east slope of Citadel Hill, overlooking the town centre. The clock's works, ordered from England, were installed in 1803. It has been chiming the quarter hour ever since and is open to the public.

The Town Clock is a landmark on the southeast slope of Citadel Hill

Chapter 2

A SOLDIER'S LIFE IN THE HALIFAX CITADEL

The Duke of Wellington called the British soldier of his day the "scum of the earth." An iron discipline maintained by flogging made for a harsh life. Soldiers were crowded into dimly lit and poorly ventilated barrack rooms with a urine tub in the centre that also served for bathing. Disease, drunkenness and desertion were the besetting evils. Infantry regiments in particular suffered from high rates of sickness and desertion. By the middle of the 19th century, however, reforms to improve diet, sanitation and barrack accommodation of the British soldier were already underway, but graphic portrayal of the appalling conditions and mal-administration during the Crimean War had a dramatic impact on British society. In this, Florence Nightingale, whom the wounded called "The Lady with the Lamp" from her nightly rounds caring for them, led public opinion in demanding action to improve conditions for soldiers.

Arthur Wellesley, First Duke of Wellington (1769-1852)
Portrait by Sir Thomas Lawrence. 1814

Of these reforms, most important were the introduction of regimental canteens, the end of corporal punishment, increasing the barrack space allotted to individual soldiers and improved food preparation. Regimental canteens, such as that of the 78th Highlanders established in the Citadel's west front, replaced those kept by private contractors who had mostly supplied hard drink, contributing greatly to deplorable drunkenness, the curse of garrison life.

Under regimental administration, canteens became comfortable and respectable places with reading material and various games, and places where soldiers could enjoy well-prepared food and beer. For the Citadel, Oland and Sons provided beer in barrels, which were stored in a tap room and brought up by beer engines. The

Citadel's canteen also sold groceries to be cooked in barracks.

Profits from the canteen went to a variety of purposes from purchasing newspapers and sports equipment to the annual Christmas dinner. In case of the 97th Regiment in garrison from 1876 to 1880 (whose Canteen Letter Book has survived), funds were used to provide men of the regiment with fur gloves for winter wear and white buff card-cases for the band, while the regimental butchers were clothed in serge suits and the letter carrier got a new bag. These purchases by the 97th were made possible by a 20 percent markup, but the popularity among the troops of the canteen may best be gauged by profits that reached £700 in 1879.

By the 1860s in the Halifax garrison, flogging, a most frightful punishment, had all but been completely replaced by detention in barracks or in military prisons. Soldiers convicted of serious offences, by court martial, could serve between 28 days and two years in military prisons. For lesser offences, they could be confined up to 28 days in garrison cells, located in the southwest demi-bastion. This could be

accompanied by hard labour, such as stone breaking. Confinement of prisoners ceased in 1857 when the army constructed a military prison on Melville Island, on the western side of the North West Arm.

Barrack Room Life

As well as the Citadel, there were other barracks in the city, the largest being Wellington Barracks near the dockyard. Such was the size of the garrison that there remained, however, a shortage of barrack space and considerable overcrowding. It was not until 1860 that the military staff could report that this problem had been overcome with 536 all-ranks and 38 women accommodated in the Citadel.

Military regulations strictly governed barrack room furnishings and utensils. Each occupant was issued an iron bedstead, an earthenware basin, two blankets, two sheets and a counterpane or, in lieu of, a third blanket, a pillow and a

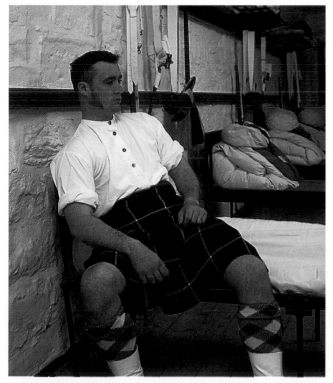

Relaxing in the barracks

The soldiers slept and ate in the Barrack Room. Both the stove and the fireplace helped keep out the cold and damp.

paillasse, both filled with straw, and a set of dishes and eating utensils. In addition, for the barrack room, there was a soldiers' table, six by four feet, with long benches for each side, and an iron stove for which one bushel of coal per day was issued to each casemate. The casemates were originally heated by fireplaces. These proved inadequate and stoves were added to improve the comfort of the soldiers. Dampness and ventilation were continuous problems. Still, and most surprisingly, medical staff reported in 1876 that the troops occupying casemates in the Citadel proved to be more healthy than those occupying rooms in regular barracks, "even though the general conditions of casemated rooms would not appear to favour this result."

Whether in a casemate or separate barrack building, barrack rooms in the Victorian army were remarkably similar.

Walls were whitewashed and the floor bare boards. With their heads against the walls, the iron bedsteads were made in two parts so that during the day one half could be folded up to create more space for the table and benches. If regulations were adhered to, there would have been space of around three feet between bedsteads. A hanging shelf over the table held all the plates and utensils. After kerosene became available, lamps using "Albertine" oil were issued. The name derived from Abraham Gesner's success in extracting kerosene from coal found in Albert County, New Brunswick.

All around the room, over the heads of beds, were shelves with hooks just below to hold all of each soldier's worldly possessions, to be maintained with scrupulous tidiness. On any spare piece of wall above his cot, he could hang pictures to give the room a more comfortable appearance. All in all,

Soldiers' wives lived in barracks with their husbands and carried out domestic tasks

however, it was fairly Spartan existence.

Military regulations allowed for only six soldiers per company to be accompanied by wives and their lives were harsh indeed. Married soldiers and their wives and children were forced to live in corners of barrack rooms with not much more than a makeshift partition separating them from the single soldiers, whose language and behaviour left much to be desired. By 1869 the Glacis Married Quarters on the east side of the Citadel were finished, providing more suitable accommodation. However, well into the 1870s a small number of non-commissioned officers' families were still living in Citadel casemates.

In the Victorian army there were no mess halls, though there were regimental kitchens. At the Citadel, after the

Cavalier Block was completed, four small casemates were added, in pairs at each end of the building, and at right angles to the existing casemates, to provide cooking facilities. On a daily rotational basis in each casemate, an orderly was appointed from among the privates. He was excused from all parades so that he could collect the rations from stores, take them to the barrack room for preparation (peeling potatoes etc.), then take them to the cook house for cooking, and afterwards return to the barrack room with the food. He was responsible for the housekeeping of the room in general. The table was constructed so that the top could be turned over: one side was hand-scrubbed to perfection. Known as the "the extra clean side" it was used only on special occasions, such as for Saturday morning room inspections. At all meals the other side would be used.

Although from mid-century on determined efforts were made to improve food preparation and provide variety, the diet remained fairly standard. Breakfast consisted of tea and bread. For dinner, the major meal of the day, eaten between 12:30 and 1:00, meat and potatoes was usual fare. Later in the afternoon there would be tea. Groceries and condiments could be purchased from the regimental canteen to give some variety. As well, the regimental cooks had a manual, *Instructions to Military Cooks*, which provided numerous recipes for meat dishes, soups and puddings.

78th Highlander family

Garrisoning An Empire

All these efforts to improve conditions for the soldier did help in recruiting. And finding suitable recruits to garrison an expanding empire remained a major concern. Soldiers of Queen Victoria could expect to spend most of their service overseas in various colonial stations. Garrisons were to be found on every continent — in India, Hong Kong, Australia, West Africa, Ionian Islands, Malta, Gibraltar, South Africa, the West Indies and so on around the globe. Steamships allowed for scheduled rotations and regiments moved every two to four years. In the second half of the 19th century, to man Halifax's garrison, 32 regiments came and went, including the 78th Highlanders.

Colours of the 78th Highland Regiment

Rank badge

Drum major in full dress

Arrival of the 78th Highlanders (Ross-shire Buffs)

On May 14, 1869 at 2:30 in the afternoon, the troopship *Crocodile* steamed into Halifax Harbour. One newspaper reported that she resembled "an enormous floating city." Aboard were 752 privates and non-commissioned officers of the 78th, accompanied by 65 wives and 140 children. Among the 29 officers, only three had wives with them.

The 78th was the first Highland regiment to be stationed in Halifax since the departure of the Black Watch in 1852 and it attracted more attention than usual.

Newspaper reports were most complimentary of the "fine body of men," noting that the kilt and tartan made a pleasing and novel con-trast to the plain scarlet

Bonnet badge of the 78th shows an elephant that commemorates service in India

Military drills are enacted daily in the Citadel during the summer

to which Haligonians had become so accustomed. Even the Baptist *Christian Messenger* commented that the regiment had made quite a sensation among the juveniles with the kilts and handsome plumes worn by the Highlanders walking about the streets.

One of only seven Highland regiments in the British army wearing the kilt, the 78th had been raised in 1793 by Francis Humberston MacKenzie, chief of Clan MacKenzie, at the outset of the war with revolutionary France. Recruits came largely from the counties of Ross and Cromarty and the island of Lewis in the West Highlands. They wore the MacKenzie tartan, and the regimental motto *Cuidich'n Righ,* Gaelic for "Save the King," was that of the Clan MacKenzie. As well, the regiment's armorial emblem, *caber feidh,* came

from the MacKenzies. It meant "deer's antlers," and it originated in the 13th century when a clan chief saved the life of his king who was being attacked by an infuriated stag. He killed the animal with a blow just behind the antlers. Its motto was emblazoned beneath the stag's head on the regimental badge and was inscribed on its colours. The 78th remained the single regiment within the British army to have Gaelic on its colours. All ranks wore red doublets with buff (tan coloured) facings, except the pipers, who dressed in green doublets.

Its fighting reputation had preceded the 78th to Halifax. It had covered itself with glory during the Indian Mutiny of 1857, leading the final charge for the relief of Lucknow, considered "one of the most famous sieges in the annals of British military history." Among those now coming to Halifax was Surgeon Valentine Macmaster, who wore the Victoria Cross that was awarded to the regiment for valour in this campaign. In one of those chance coincidences of history, the commander at Lucknow during the 87-day siege was a native Haligonian, John Inglis, son and grandson of two Nova Scotian bishops, who became known as the "Hero of Lucknow" and received a knighthood. Alfred Lord Tennyson commemorated the 78th's deeds in his poem *Defence of Lucknow*:

*Surely the pibroch of Europe is
    ringing again in our ears!
All on a sudden the garrison
    utter a jubilant shout,
Havelock's glorious Highlanders
    answer with conquering cheers,
Sick from the hospital echo them,
    women and children come out,
Kissing the war-hardened hand
    of the Highlander wet with
    their tears
Dance to the pibroch!— is it you?
    is it you?*

When, in 1860, after 17 years service in India, the regiment returned to Scotland, a crowd of 60,000 turned out to greet the heroes of Lucknow. The regiment remained in Great Britain and Gibraltar for the next six years before being sent to Montreal in 1867 and two years later to Halifax.

Pipers in the 78th played specific tunes for events such as reveille, retreat and lights out

Settling In

Regiments like the 78th looked upon themselves as a family and the regiment their home. Many would spend a good part of their lives with their regiment. Lieutenant Colonel Alexander Mackenzie, commanding officer of the 78th while in Halifax, had become an ensign in 1840 and would serve in it for the next 32 years. During the Indian Mutiny he had seen much action, was wounded twice and commended for his resolution and courage. For a bachelor with only modest financial means, the 78th was truly his life.

In the Victorian army, regiments formed the basic fighting unit and their structure was designed to make them administratively largely self-sufficient. Within the 78th, responsibility for daily administration rested with Lieutenant Charles Croker-King, the adjutant,

Undress or working uniform

and the Regimental Sergeant Major: Alexander Macdonald until 1870 and then Parr Campbell. As well as a paymaster, a surgeon and an assistant surgeon, both of whom had to be graduates of one of the Royal Colleges of Surgeons of London, Edinburgh or Dublin, there was a regimental tailor, a regimental schoolmaster and a schoolmistress.

Schoolmasters had to be graduates of the army's Normal School and taught the children of soldiers on the regiment's

strength. As promotion for privates and non-commissioned officers depended on obtaining various educational levels, the schoolmaster held after-duty classes for them. Each Christmas day the schoolmaster would show comic slides to the garrison children using the regiment's magic lantern.

Regimental Schools

Regimental schools proved to be among the more significant reforms introduced during the 19th century. Attendance for all children of married soldiers up to the age of 14 became compulsory. Interestingly for the period, the army prohibited the use of punishment by masters. Each regiment had a schoolmaster and a schoolmistress and engaged other staff to assist as needed. When the 78th arrived in Halifax, Crawford Flemming was the schoolmaster and Elizabeth Ross the schoolmistress.

The schoolmaster had responsibility for the Adult and Grown Children's School. Flemming would have held classes six days a week, with a three-week summer holiday. Both the adults and children attended school from 9:00 a.m. until noon. In the afternoon the two groups returned at different times for an hour's instruction. The three Rs – reading, writing and arithmetic – formed the core of the curriculum. Students practised penmanship and writing in lined copybooks and did rudimentary mathematics on slate and in books. Writing included composition, transcribing from the blackboard and taking oral dictation. Students demonstrated their reading ability by reading aloud.

Elizabeth Ross, a single woman and one of only 24 out of 225 schoolmistresses in the Army's employ who had the highest level of teaching certification, divided her time between the Infant School in the morning and the Industrial School in the afternoon. As regulations meant that all students could attend, the Infant School provided nursery care to allow mothers to work at laundry and other chores. Usually, on reaching seven or eight years of age, children went on to the schoolmaster's school. In the afternoon grown girls could attend the Industrial School, where they learned domestic skills. Although there was a considerable advocacy for boys' industrial schools, the army did not introduce them.

Andrew McEleney, bandmaster

Attendance could be erratic, particularly for soldiers, but Schoolmaster Flemming, who had three assistants, could have almost 400 students in his classes. At the Infant School, Elizabeth Ross had about 40 young children to teach and care for. Flemming also delivered lectures during the winter months on a wide variety of historical, scientific and geographical subjects. For these he had the use of the garrison's magic lantern, a precursor of the modern slide projector. Today, a magic lantern can be seen on display in the Regimental Schoolroom located in a casemate off the South Parade.

Regimental Band, Fifers and Drummers and Pipers

Highland regiments had a regimental band, a corps of 21 drummers, fifers and buglers, and five pipers. The director of the 78th regimental band was Bandmaster Sergeant Andrew McEleney, a graduate of the Royal School of Music at Kneller Hall. The drummers, buglers and fifers came under the charge of Drum Major George Taylor to 1870 and then of Alexander Cardy. When the regiment paraded, the Drum Major marched "baton in hand, at the head of the regiment in order to give time to the band." Ten of the corps played the drums, while 10 were buglers, who also played the fife, so that a fife and drum band could be formed. All regiments, including the Highland, drilled to the fife and drum because battalions needed to manoeuvre on the battlefield with disciplined precision.

Buglers were required to be familiar with all army bugle calls, which they played to indicate duties required or events to take place. All ranks had to be able to identify each of the myriad calls being blown, because the bugle regulated all ordinary garrison life. Bugle calls summoned men to parades and duties, or when rations were ready for collecting, for instance. Pipers in the 78th, however, played particular tunes for such events as reveille (*Johnny Cope*), dress for parade (*MacKenzie Highlanders*), retreat (*Sir Colin Campbell*) and lights out (*Soldier Lie Down on a Wee Pickle Straw*).

All line regiments had drum majors and a corps of drummers, fifers and buglers, but unique to Highland regiments

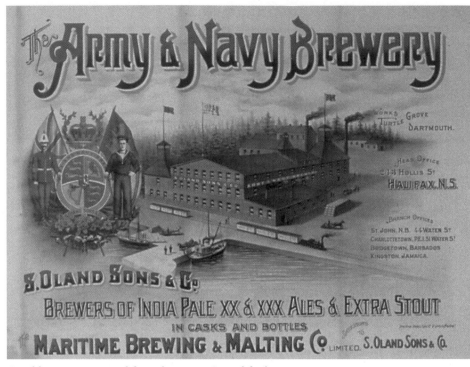

Local breweries prospered from the garrison's need for beer

were pipe majors who had charge of the regimental corps of five pipers, which regulations allowed them to carry on their strength. While in Halifax, Ronald Mackenize was pipe major. He had joined the regiment in 1860, the year after he had won "at the great northern meeting, the Dirk, Gold Medal, and Set of Pipes in open competition." He became pipe major in 1863 and was "long regarded as one of the best pipers of his day."

A Routine Day with the 78th Highlanders in the Citadel

For all ranks of the 78th, garrison life centred on the Citadel, where most of the regiment lived. Although numbers varied, generally around 300 privates had their barracks in 26 casemates (10 to 12 in each) in the west and north fronts and in the Cavalier Building. Officers' quarters were in the redan. A number of married non-commissioned officers had separate casemates given to them, but by the 78th's tour all married

soldiers with their wives and children lived in married quarters in the city, as it had become no longer acceptable to having them share casemates with single men. Remaining casemates were used for the regimental canteen, officers' and sergeants' messes, a library, a recreational room, cookhouses, privies, wash rooms, school room, tailor shop, shoemaker shop, pay office, quartermaster stores and so on.

From May to September regimental pipers sounded reveille at 5:30 (in winter at 6:30). After dressing, the men would double up their cots and arrange their paillasses, pillows and blankets in the regulation manner. Next they would pay a visit to the ablution room in the north end of the Citadel, where they could have a quick, cold, early morning wash. An hour after reveille came the first parade of the day, which consisted of physical exercises for 20 minutes and 10 minutes of running drill.

Upon dismissal, the men returned to their barrack rooms for a breakfast of tea and bread. In the two hours before the main parade of the day, they would carry out "soldiering" tasks, cleaning kit, shining boots, polishing brass and pipe-claying accoutrements. Special attention would be paid to ensure the room was neat and kit laid out according to regulations. An officer inspected barrack rooms each day with a major inspection on Saturday mornings.

For the 10 o'clock parade, troops dressed in full marching order wearing red doublets and feather bonnets, with their knapsacks containing the approved field kit. For the next hour on the parade square, under either the adjutant or regimental sergeant major, companies, of which there were 10, went through battle drills. On the last day of the month, this parade became a muster parade with the commanding officer present. All ranks, regardless of their duties as grooms, tailors,

Soldiers' smoking room (1872)

shoemakers etc., had to attend. After parade, the men returned to their barrack rooms to complete any further soldiering tasks.

At noon, the regimental canteen opened, and a pint of beer could be had before dinner. Last parade of the day came at two o'clock, lasted for 30 minutes and then, for those men not on guard, fatigue or work details, the day was finished. Most would stay in the Citadel until tea at four o'clock. Both the regimental canteen and the recreation room in the northeast front were open, but a good many would head out of the Citadel for the well-known "attractions" of Victorian Halifax.

On Sunday, the morning was taken up with the required Church Parade. Since 1846 the garrison had had its own chapel where most of the garrison attended. Before the 78th arrived in Halifax, Colonel Mackenzie had written ahead to Reverend George Monro Grant (later to be principal of Queen's University at Kingston, Ontario), of St. Matthew's

Presbyterian Church at the bottom of Spring Garden Road, that 450 of the regiment were Presbyterians.

As it turned out, St. Matthew's had to provide Grant with an assistant because of this dramatic increase in the congregation and a third Sunday service had to be instituted. In 1870 the congregation purchased the discharge of Sergeant John Cook so it could hire him to lead the congregation in singing. When also the congregation temporarily needed a choir, it engaged the choir of the 78th.

Troops from the different barracks marched, led by their bands, to the Garrison Chapel and other churches with side arms only. The parade to the churches was a popular weekly event. Crowds would form on the sidewalks and follow the troops. Garrison chaplains, anyway, had the reputation of being good preachers, though on the firing of the noon gun it was understood any sermon would come to an abrupt finish. As well as an organ, military bands and string instruments provided the music at the Garrison Chapel. After services the troops marched back to barracks accompanied by crowds of onlookers. As they reached their respective barracks, the bands would play the regimental marches until parade dismissal. After Church Parade, the remainder of the day was free of military parades until Retreat.

At 9:30 in the evening (in winter, an hour earlier), the evening gun was fired, signalling all soldiers to return to barracks. Between the evening gun and the sounding of the last post a half hour later on the Parade Square, regimental pipers or buglers and drummers on duty performed the time-honoured ceremony of beating the Retreat, or Tattoo as the ceremony is more commonly known.

Its origins lay in 17th-century Holland, where at the time of Retreat, drummers paraded through the streets to warn publicans to turn off the beer taps and soldiers to return to their quarters. The word tattoo derives from the Flemish *Doe Den Tap Toe*, meaning literally "Turn off the Taps," which British soldiers anglicized into tattoo. In the Halifax garrison the ceremony usually consisted of three lively tunes with intervals in between, the last one seguing into "God Save the Queen." This nightly ceremony could be heard over much of the city. Over time the tattoo has evolved into a form of spectacular entertainment involving military bands and performers. Since 1979 the Nova Scotia International Tattoo, employing a mixture of military and civilian performers, has been performing annually to tens of thousands.

Once back inside the Citadel, soldiers formed up in their respective companies

Members of the animation group march from the Citadel to their guard post at Government House on Barrington Street

The pipe band at the Citadel performs regularly in the summer months

for "tattoo roll-call." Company orderly sergeants read out the name of each man. When there was no reply, he was reported absent without leave. The names of those absent were reported to the guard commander who was responsible for going in search of them. At 10 o'clock the last post sounded, formally ending the military day. "Lights out" followed 15 minutes later.

Guard Duties, Route Marches and the Queen's Birthday

For the private soldier of the 78th Highlanders, the most onerous of his duties in peace time garrison life was that of guard duty. Every day the regiment provided guards for seven military establishments in the city. Privates did the actual standing guard, with two hours on and four hours off for a full 24-hour period. Guards had to remain fully dressed throughout their detachment's tour of duty. For shifts outside the Citadel, such as at the Ordnance Yard on Water Street (just north of present-day Historic Properties), the respective guards formed up for inspection on the Parade Square before marching out at 10 a.m. and parading along Halifax's streets in full marching order, dropping off individual detachments as they moved from post to post, the last being Government House, opposite the Old Burial Ground.

As well as the daily guard duties, detachments were sent for longer periods to man the signal stations at Sambro and Camperdown. During the time of the 78th, an electric telegraph connected Camperdown to the Citadel, ending the need for the visual telegraph established by Prince Edward in the 1790s. Another detachment lived in the Martello Tower at Point Pleasant Park, which had been converted into a site for ammunition storage. Troops from the Halifax garrison were also sent on a rotational basis to Fredericton, New

Parade outside the Garrison Chapel

Brunswick, to serve as a small garrison.

During the summer months, companies engaged in musketry training at the newly established rifle range in Bedford, outside of Halifax. Winter, however, could be an especially monotonous time for a garrison. The regiment donned winter uniforms with great coats and trews, trousers made by the regimental tailor from old kilts. At least once a week during the winter months the full regiment went on a route march, usually to Point Pleasant Park, led by the Regimental Band. There, weapons could be fired and sham battles staged. By the time the 78th arrived in Halifax, Point Pleasant was in the process of becoming a public park under an arrangement whereby the military turned over the land to Halifax on a 999-year lease for the annual sum of one shilling, on the

express condition that it could continue to be used for military purposes and repossessed if needed. Annually, at a special ceremony in June, the park's appointed commissioners still pay over the sum of one shilling to the Crown.

For the garrison, winter ended and spring really began with the celebrations marking Queen Victoria's birthday on May 24 every year. On the North Common would be a grand military display involving all the garrison and whatever naval ships were in port. For the 78th Highlanders' first May 24 in Halifax, the *Evening Reporter* noted that participation by the regiment had aroused great interest. At quarter to 12 on that morning with the whole garrison in double line, Major General Sir Hasting Doyle arrived to take the salute and carry out his inspection. Then on the firing of the noon gun, cannon from the naval ships roared forth, followed by other batteries of the city defences. Then came a *feu de joie* down the front rank and up the rear rank by the members of the 78th with their recently issued Snider-Enfield breech-loading rifles. Hasting Doyle called for three cheers for the Queen. After forming open columns, the troops marched off, giving a display of marching time led by bands. Our reporter noted that "the sprightly step of the Highlanders, and the physique of all the troops was on everybody's tongue, and a large number of 'Uncle Sam's sons,' who were present, were evidently impressed with the show."

As the Queen's birthday was a public holiday, once the troops returned to barracks, the remainder of the day was theirs. Public holidays free of all parades were the religious days of Christmas, Ash Wednesday, Good Friday and Easter. Holidays also fell on the dates of the Queen's coronation and the Prince of Wales's birthday. The Royal Standard always flew from the Citadel's flag staff on these occasions. But for the 78th, as true Scots, the chief holiday was New Year's or hogmanay, as it is still called in Scotland, when the regimental cooks served haggis, accompanied no doubt by goodly amounts of scotch whisky. A holiday unique to the Halifax garrison was the city's Natal Day held on June 21. Orders of the day provided for the Citadel to be thrown open to visitors from noon to six in the evening with the flag staff gaily decorated for the occasion.

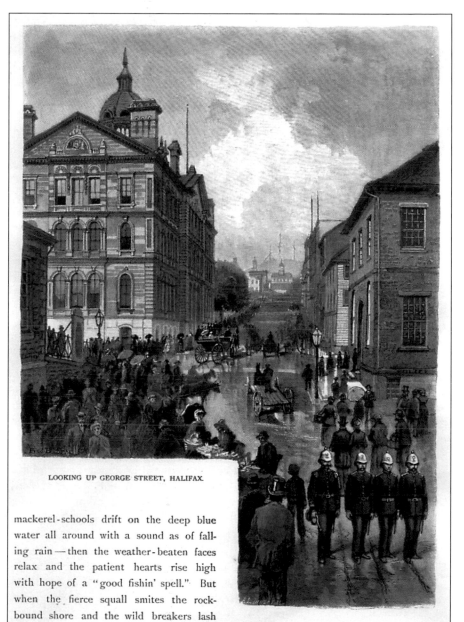

LOOKING UP GEORGE STREET, HALIFAX.

mackerel-schools drift on the deep blue water all around with a sound as of falling rain — then the weather-beaten faces relax and the patient hearts rise high with hope of a "good fishin' spell." But when the fierce squall smites the rockbound shore and the wild breakers lash it with resistless force, many a deeply-laden boat is swept to its destruction; many

Page from Picturesque Canada *shows the view up George Street in the late 19th century, from Cheapside to the Citadel.*

Chapter 3

IMPERIAL TOWN AND GARRISON

Of all the major military stations outside Great Britain, Halifax ranked by far as the most popular among regiments. Gibraltar was considered no better than a prison. Malta was not much more agreeable with its terrific heat and unending boredom. Although over time conditions did improve in the West Indies and Bermuda, they remained among the most detested stations, with a continuing high mortality rate. Halifax's more congenial climate compared to service in the tropics remained an important reason that regiments favoured this station. For private soldiers and commanding officers alike, Halifax had much to offer for breaking the sheer boredom of daily garrison existence.

Drawing of Halifax from across the harbour (William Eagar) (1837)

Horse-racing (above) and sleigh rides (below) on the Halifax Common were popular pastimes for soldiers and civilians

Although Victorian Halifax had a notorious underworld of taverns and brothels on Barrack Street just below Citadel Hill and on adjoining streets, those soldiers seeking better society could and did find it. Numbers of soldiers became stalwart members of temperance societies, which, as the century progressed, became increasing influential and social. James Potter of the 78th became a temperance advocate, took his discharge in Halifax and was engaged by St. Matthew's as its city missionary. Later he became a church elder. As well, from the 1860s on, soldiers engaged in sports and other forms of recreation.

For the Leninsters (Royal Canadians), Halifax remained "the only decent station on the colonial tour." On its departure in 1886, after three years in garrison, Halifax for the Royal Irish Rifles "had been a delightful station and all were sorry to leave it, the men especially so." Lieutenant Frederick Harris Veith believed, during his tour in the late 1850s, that for the number of pretty girls, Halifax "brilliantly outshone... any city of its size, anywhere." A Royal Artillery officer commented on the Halifax of the 1860s:

The population is more English in manners and ideas than any other I have met in America... The labouring classes are respectable, and, as a rule, well-to-do; the trading part of the inhabitants are well-informed, civil and honest; and the professions are represented by men who have had an education far superior to most colonies and many districts of England.

A general prosperity marked these years before Confederation, in part due to the reciprocity treaty with the United States, which, however, the United States unilaterally repealed in 1866. Of Halifax's population of 28,000, a high proportion were Nova Scotian born, generally going back many generations. Commerce with a little manufacturing formed the base of Halifax's economy. The West Indian trade remained a mainstay for the merchants of Water Street. From the Naval Dockyard in the north along Water Street to near Point Pleasant Park lay a sea of wharves and a forest of masts. But dramatic change came with steamships and railways. With Confederation in 1867 came the Intercolonial Railway and Halifax's determination to become the winter port for the new Dominion of Canada. Halifax's civic landscape reflected this change with the construction of a major railway station, a grain elevator, steamship terminus and a dry dock that was the largest facility of its type on the Atlantic seaboard, used even by American battleships.

Halifax also benefited greatly from British military expenditures. Although the cost for constructing the Citadel had come to £243,122, this figure had not included the amount for paying and maintaining the garrison. General Sir Hasting

Doyle estimated that keeping the garrison in Halifax for the 1860s cost around £300,000 annually. Then there was the massive rearmament programme between 1863 and 1873 with the construction of new forts and the mounting of rifled muzzle loaders. Its cost came to £265,000, much of which was spent in Halifax.

Just provisioning the garrison alone involved purchases from 50 suppliers. A chief supplier was the Moir and Son Bakery, which still survives as a well-known maker of chocolates. To ensure impartiality and good service, five companies in each trade were given one-year contracts on the basis of tenders. As well, provisions, coal, seal oil, animal forage and the hire of carters were just a few of the other items to be supplied. Such brewers as Oland and Son and Alexander Keith did handsomely from the sale of beers and ales. Even by 1904, with a much reduced garrison, expenditures still amounted to £211,000.

A further benefit came from increased tourism. By 1882, estimates for American tourists alone coming to Halifax were as many as 2,000 with the Citadel and garrison of major interest. Colourful military tournaments and trooping of the colour ceremonies proved exciting attractions, as they

The garrison soldiers provided entertainment for young ladies in Halifax on long winter nights

still do with the Nova Scotia International Tattoo an annual event.

Pleasures of Halifax Society

Although throughout the 19th century Halifax's commercial fortunes ebbed and flowed, military expenditures remained a fairly constant source of income. There was more wealth in Halifax than met the eye and a more lively social scene than appearances might suggest. Victorian society had a God-fearing, highly moralist religious tone to it, but this should not lead us to believe Victorians did not enjoy themselves. Whether of town or garrison, citizen or soldier, they found their pleasures in myriad activities and entertainments.

Coasting on Citadel Hill was a popular winter pastime

In summer, picnics to such places as McNabs Island and Prince's Lodge by yacht were much approved of by the younger set. The prevailing wind from the west had a tendency, almost invariably, to drop before sundown, so the voyage home could take much longer than fretting chaperones thought proper. There were also archery and croquet in the Halifax Public Gardens, aquatic carnivals in the harbour, yacht racing and boating on the North West Arm, canoeing on the Dartmouth Lakes, shooting at the new Bedford Rifle Range, horse racing on the commons and so on.

During the long dreary winter months town and garrison avidly enjoyed such amusements as skating parties at the rink inside the Public Gardens (the first covered rink in Canada) or on nearby lakes. When Maynard's Lake froze solid in the winter of 1870, hundreds crossed to Dartmouth on the ferry to enjoy the skating, while the band of the 78th Regiment "discoursed sweet music." The *Acadian Recorder* reported that

the "wealth and beauty of Halifax were fully represented and the scene was one of the rarest and most exhilarating description." Skating carnivals were regular events for which the garrison bands provided the music and all ranks participated.

Every good snowfall brought out the horse-drawn sleighs. Many garrison officers purchased sleighs during their Halifax tour. A favourite among the usual 30 or 40 bachelors in the garrison were excursions to Bedford with their belles, warmly wrapped in bearskin and buffalo robes, for dinner and impromptu dances, returning by moonlight to the sound of sleigh bells.

Sometimes accidents could happen, as when Ensign George Callander of the 78th was showing off his driving skills to one of Alexander Keith's four daughters, only to have his horses bolt. He was thrown out of the sleigh and Miss Keith, horse and sleigh, crashed into a dry goods store. Fortunately, a surgeon from the Royal Artillery was passing and determined her injuries were not serious. Callander was

Members of the garrison often staged plays and pantomimes

the 17th Regiment performed *Visions of Christmas* (adapted from Charles Dickens's *A Christmas Carol*) and a pantomime for the benefit of Halifax's poor. Plays performed were almost always of a moral nature with such titles as *Maid of Genoa, The Haunted Inn, Black-eyed Susan, High Life Below Stairs, Post of Honour* and *Poor Pillicoddy* in which the good were duly rewarded and the wicked properly chastised. As many as three such plays could be performed for an evening's entertainment, lasting three or four hours. Locales varied from Government House to theatres where touring companies performed and the Garrison Recreational Building.

believed to have been driving too fast. There is reason to believe Alexander Keith was not amused and the charming Miss Keith had to look elsewhere for a beau. But such could be the damnable luck of a courting subaltern.

Throughout the winter there would be no shortage of dinners, dances and little entertainments held in regimental messes or in the private houses of the wealthy, many of whom had their residences and estates overlooking the North West Arm, with such engaging names as Oaklands, Belmont and Rosebank. At mid-century in Halifax, the quadrille was still the most popular dance, involving four couples in a square formation performing intertwining figures. But the waltz, with its turning, embracing couples, which had initially so shocked polite society, gained increasing favour.

To relieve winter's dreary nights, garrison officers performed amateur theatrics and civilians often joined them. Performances could be public or private and be staged for amusement or various charitable causes, as when members of

Soldiers from the garrison formed a very high proportion of the audiences for both professional touring companies and amateur theatricals. Between 1850 and 1880 there were 3,000 individual performances in the city by 41 touring companies and an estimated 50 amateur groups, the majority of whom came from the garrison, whose thespian efforts did much to relieve the tedium of a Halifax winter. The touring companies tended to be small in numbers and often required assistance from willing amateurs.

For the performance of the highly popular Victorian "potboiler" *Jessie Brown, or the Relief of Lucknow*, the company called on the services of a number of the 78th Highlanders for a Halifax performance in 1870. In the play, when all seemed lost, and just when British soldiers were to shoot all the women so they might avoid a fate worse than death, the relieving force of the Highlanders burst onto the stage.

However, on this occasion the Highlanders had been too well treated beforehand and became "so hot" that they actually began clubbing the shocked mutineers with their muskets, bloodying a number. Others, in climbing over the stage wall to rescue the besieged, got their kilts caught on the joints holding the wall together and could not free themselves. A grinny old woman, who sold apples and oranges in front of the stage, cried out at the top of her voice: "Yah! Yah! why do ye no pull down yer kilties, instead o' kicken' there? Yah! Yer no decent — do yer hear?" All Halifax now knew "what a Scotsman wore under his kilt."

Under much different circumstances, Pipe Major Mackenzie and regimental pipers were often called upon to perform at such events as the Grand Celtic Concert or in the Public Gardens. Pipe Major Mackenzie would perform the sword dance for which he became noted while in Halifax, and pipers would dance reels and highland flings.

The summer social season began with the arrival, around May 24, of the Naval Squadron from its Bermuda winter station. With the season came "little picnics à deux" and other such secluded assignations. No regiment would depart without its share of marriages to Halifax girls. In the case of the 78th, three of its officers married into Halifax's merchant elite with no doubt suitable dowries forthcoming. When Surgeon Valentine Macmaster, V.C., married Annie Burmester at St. Paul's in June 1870, "the ancient edifice was crowned with the beauty and fashion of the city," with the bride attended by six bridesmaids, and the groom by officers of the 78th in full dress. Among the rank and file for some regiments, up to 100 men might get married to local girls during a tour of duty.

Public Spectacles

Perhaps such marriages were due to the attraction of handsome uniforms and manly bearing. Haligonians certainly turned out in the thousands for public spectacles put on by the garrison. Royal Visits were great occasions and that of Prince Arthur in August 1869 proved to be such an event. Nineteen years old and the third son of Queen Victoria and Prince Albert, Arthur would later return to Canada as Governor General from 1911 to 1916.

Before his arrival, the whole garrison lined the streets, to greet the then-Governor General, Sir John Young, and the Minister of Militia and Defence, George Etienne Cartier, who arrived from Ottawa by train. As the regal party passed, each unit presented arms and the band played a march, until it reached Government House, where the 78th gave the final present. That evening the 78th's band provided music for a grand dinner of seven courses. For the occasion, Bandmaster Andrew McEleney composed a quadrille *Cuidich'n Righ* (the 78th's motto).

No royal visit could pass without a full military review, which took place four days after Prince Arthur's arrival. After an inspection by Prince Arthur and a march past, the troops deployed for a sham battle, which newspapers reported in great detail and florid prose:

Government House by J.E. Woolford (1819)

The bugle sounds the advance and at the same time the skirmishers open fire...the line opens fire, and for a minute or two there is one deafening roar of musketry. The skirmish line retires, and the order to charge is given...and again the line halts and again it fires a deafening volley...The second line of the attack consisting of the sailors and the 78th Highlanders, then advances, and goes through similar maneuvers...[then] the order 'prepare to receive cavalry' is given. Squares are immediately formed, and firing commences again....

After this last manoeuvre, and with the enemy presumably defeated, the troops reformed and marched off.

Garrison officers held a ball for Prince Arthur, for which the Royal Engineers were fully employed in the preceding two weeks decorating Province House. Above the stairway leading to the dance floor, the Engineers suspended a gigantic moose head to represent the 78th's emblem, surrounded by evergreens with the regimental motto suitably inscribed. It proved to be the most glittering social event of the year with one newspaper commenting on how it amusing it was to see some of the Highland officers "dancing as if they were in the middle of a war dance." When Prince Arthur embarked at the end of the five-day visit, the 78th provided an 80-man guard of honour with the Queen's Colour on parade.

Of Queen Victoria's long reign, no occasion would be more celebrated and with more fervent loyalty by town and garrison than her Diamond Jubilee of 1897. A splendid military tournament held in the Exhibition Building, under the patronage of the visiting Governor General Lord Aberdeen, initiated the festivities on June 19. It began with an opening march by the band of the Royal Berkshire Regiment, followed by bayonet exercises, gymnastics, cutlass drill, acrobatics, gun shifting and club swinging. In a tug of war, men from the Berkshires pulled 10 sailors from the *Crescent* in a record time of 16.5 seconds.

As a finale, a sham war was staged. British infantry came under fire unexpectedly by a force of Afghans, who then retreated to a realistic fort constructed at the north end of the rink. After Engineers and naval crewmen built a bridge across a river, the infantry, firing a fusillade, advanced to the fort. Once the Engineers blew up the gates, the Afghans were taken prisoners. During the week the tournament was repeated on a number of occasions with as many as 3,000 attending a showing.

On the great holiday of June 22, it proved to be "queen's weather." First came the military review on the Common, watched by some 25,000. At noon that day, Royal Artillery fired a Royal Salute from Citadel Hill, replied to by a 60-gun salute from the *Crescent* in the harbour. Well before sunset spectators crowded Citadel Hill and around a big square laid out on the North Common for the tattoo ceremony. After a display of rockets, bugles blew tattoo at 9:30. As soon as the music died away, soldiers lighted hundreds of Chinese lanterns and then marched and countermarched to music to the delight of the spectators. After the band played "God Save the Queen," a "wonderfully arranged representation of Her Majesty's face surrounded by all colours of pretty lights could be seen in the sky and the spontaneous roar 'left no doubt of the loyalty of Halifax.'"

From Cricket to Ricket to Hockey

In its October 17, 1786 issue, the *Nova Scotia Chronicle* published an announcement for a cricket match between gentlemen of the army and navy. Although teams from within the garrison played cricket, Haligonians did not have a local team until the Mayflower Cricket Club came into being in 1842. Other clubs were formed and by the early 1860s matches between town and garrison became a regular feature of Halifax life. By Confederation, cricket was the leading sport being played in the city. Until the formation of the Phoenix Club, which took the best players from other clubs, teams from the garrison regularly defeated local clubs.

Haligonians became quite caught up in an extraordinary frenzy to see the garrison defeated by their own. The garrison's "Waterloo" finally came in 1869, when after Phoenix first defeated teams from 87th and 60th regiments, it took on the best the garrison could field. Five thousand people turned out to watch the match at the Garrison Grounds on Quinpool Road. A full military band entertained the excited throng adding to the carnival atmosphere. They were well rewarded, as the Phoenix team handed out a "sound thrashing" to the "gallant British officers." From this victory the

Officers' cricket team

Phoenix players went on to wins over the Royal Navy team and the Combined Services Eleven to end the season with an unbeaten record and become the "toast of the Province."

In 1874, Captain N.W. Wallace who, as well as being an enthusiast was a first class player, took on the task of organizing an international tournament. Invitations went out to cities in Canada and the United States. Three teams entered the tournament. To form the Canadian team, selectors took three players from Halifax with the remainder from Ontario and Quebec. From the United States came an "all-star" Philadelphia team, then the hot bed of cricket in that country. Garrison cricketers made up England's team.

Great excitement gripped Halifax, though there was disappointment when the Canadians did not make the final. For the finale, as a local newspaper described the final match, between England and America, the band of 60th Rifles first performed, while the carriage stand filled up with all kinds of "turn outs" from the humble "one horse shy" to the dashing drag and unicorn. When the Americans won the match, the *Evening Reporter* chortled that they had "usurped the position of England as Queen of Cricket," a comment that no doubt was less than well received in the officers' messes. The paper also noted that afterwards a baseball game had been played and it reported, "the general public did not seem to take much interest in it as it looked a bit slow and perhaps, we say it softly, a wee bit 'spooney' [foolish, silly]."

On the origin of hockey and where it was first played, there remains no consensus. Although various claims associate its beginnings with Imperial garrisons, there is some evidence that Mi'kmaq, living at Tufts Cove of Halifax Harbour, played a game on ice with a rounded block of wood as a puck with around eight men on each team in the eighteenth century. Our first documentary evidence on the playing of wicket or ricket on ice with skates in Halifax comes from the *Novascotian* of February 24, 1831, which noted that:

> There has been excellent skating upon the head of the North West Arm, and large parties of Towns folks and the Military, have enjoyed, during several afternoons of this and the past week, the healthy stirring game of Wicket.

Wicket, or as it was more usually called ricket or rickets, became a regular sporting activity indulged in by members of the garrison and the young men of the town when ice conditions allowed. Whether or not officers of the 78th had been introduced to ricket when stationed in Montreal, on arrival in Halifax a number joined with members of Phoenix Cricket club and another in Dartmouth to form a three-team league.

As cricketers placed wickets, ricketers placed stones on the ice for goal posts with the players using a hurley (Irish form of field hockey) stick. Any number could play and the game began by tossing a ball into the air as opposed to dropping a puck. Interestingly, cricket teams from town and garrison would play both cricket and ricket matches on ice, usually one after the other. Often on winter Saturday afternoons there would be scratch matches on the North West Arm. Where planned ahead, a military band would play for skaters and entertain during the game.

Curling was a winter sport with which Highland regiments would have been familiar before coming to Halifax. Probably a naval officer, Captain Huston Stewart, introduced curling to Haligonians during the 1820s. But it was Captain H.M. Drummond of the 42nd Highlanders (Black Watch), when his regiment was in garrison from 1851 to 1852, who "greatly stimulated" the game by his infectious enthusiasm. He became president of the Halifax Curling Club, founded in 1849. On his return to Scotland, he donated to the club "a magnificent pair of curling stones" set in silver. Known as the Drummond Stones, for many years local clubs competed annually for them. Other than this competition, it seems

teams just issued challenges when ice conditions allowed, as in 1867, when garrison officers challenged both the Thistle and Halifax Clubs to matches on the Dartmouth Lakes.

Flat Racing

A sport that brought together town and garrison in the middle years of the 19th century was that of flat racing on the North Common. After a course was marked out in 1825, civilian and military "Gentlemen Jockeys" engaged in sweepstakes, handicaps and match-races. Thousands would watch from Citadel Hill. Betting was heavy and lay at the root of a good many riots. Although it was considered too unladylike to wager money, ladies of town and garrison engaged in "glove betting," in which they laid bets with one another with I.O.U.s for pairs of gloves or boxes of candy. The first cross-country steeplechase took place in 1839, while the first steeplechase course was laid out in 1882.

Polo and Rugby

In no two sports were social distinctions more contrasting than in polo and rugby, both within the garrison and in the community at large. Only the most wealthy among the garrison officers and their civilian friends could afford polo. The first polo game in Canada took place in Halifax in 1878. A year later polo grounds were laid out and a club organized, but little polo seems to have been played until 1889 and the formation of the Halifax Polo Club, which had a rough field turned into a smooth green lawn. Games were played during the summer months on each Tuesday and Friday at 4 p.m. *The Dominion Illustrated News* believed polo was played nowhere but in Halifax, "where the presence of military and naval men gives the impetus to all manly sport." Matches attracted a large number of spectators. An active supporter of polo in Halifax was Prince George, later George V, who as a naval officer spent many enjoyable summers on station. A Governor General reported to Prime Minister Sir John A. MacDonald that the prince's presence "brings all the filles here like flies around a honey-pot."

In the late 1870s, English rugby, or football as it was then called, began to replace cricket, especially in universities, where it inspired enthusiastic displays of college spirit. Clubs in many Nova Scotia communities formed teams. Initially, not even uniforms were worn and rules were open to much debate, but this changed by the late 1880s. Football also became highly popular when travel by rail allowed teams to play in different communities.

Equally popular within the garrison, regiments organized teams. Though cricket was dominated by officers, football appealed to all, and the majority of players were drawn from other ranks. A case in point was the football club of the Duke of Wellington's Regiment, known as the The Dukes, on which there were 10 privates and non-commissioned officers compared to four officers. As well as playing such teams in Halifax as Dalhousie University in 1891, which proved to be "splendidly contested," the team travelled to Charlottetown, New Glasgow and Pictou for games. It achieved sufficient renown to have a picture of the whole team appear in the *Dominion Illustrated News*.

Such success by garrison teams proved to be short lived as local clubs like the Wanderers began fielding strong teams. At the 1897 season's opening match before a large number of spectators (league football especially attracted the ladies), the Wanderers defeated a United Services (army and navy) team by 16 to 2. Probably because of a much reduced garrison,

The Dukes, the football team of the Duke of Wellington's regiment (1891)

Garrison gymnasium or recreation room

Two Views of Town and Garrison

Francis Duncan, an officer of the Royal Artillery, wrote of Halifax in the 1860s, when comparing it to other garrison towns he had known in Britain and abroad:

... of this I can speak with certainty, that for seclusion and the absence of insult, with at the same time a full amount of the social intercourse which is necessary to the well-being of man, and to his happiness, I have never met a town in England or Scotland of its size [30,000 population] to equal it. You may enjoy, if you choose, all the calm of even some sleepy cathedral town; or you may have the quiet little dissipations, which have the pleasure with the sting of excitement, on a larger scale; or, finally – thanks in a great measure, to the garrison and the fleet – you have gaiety to a degree undreamt of in towns of the same size at home.

Dalhousie and the Wanderers began winning by wide margins over army and navy teams. By 1904, even fielding a strong United Services team proved so difficult that for one game the Navy, using Marconi's new invention of wireless communication, contacted HMS *Charybdis* at sea and ordered her to steam to Halifax with a key player. She arrived in time for him to play, but United Services, though it played a strong game, still lost.

As well as football, boxing gained much popularity in this period and garrison bouts drew large crowds. For the opening of a new garrison gymnasium in 1902, 800 attended to watch a evening of matches. Many travelled hundreds of miles. In attendance were regimental colonels, members of Parliament and civic fathers. No smoking was allowed, nor apparently were comments during bouts. Visitors from New York, Montreal and Toronto were surprised that "such a large crowd subjection [sic], with so many exciting incidents as were liable to cause an outburst" all went off without any disturbance.

In the 1880s, Sandford Fleming, chief engineer for the building of both Intercolonial and Canadian Pacific Railways, as a Halifax resident wrote of the garrison:

But when to these recognized advantages [those of nature and climate] the social elements of Halifax are added, it is held by common consent that there are few cities more attractive. And we remember the well-bred, travelled men many of whom also highly educated, to be met among the officers of the garrison and on board the ships at the station, with their efforts to return the hospitalities of the citizens, we must acknowledge that Halifax, in its social aspects, possesses features and a charm peculiar to itself.

Part 2

INTRODUCTION

The second section of this book looks at the early history of Halifax and the four forts erected on Citadel Hill. The town's *raison d'être* was as a naval base to help establish British supremacy in North America and expel the French from the region. From the first days of British settlement, the naval dockyard and the townsfolk needed fortified protection. Over the next one hundred years, three forts were built and successively fell into disrepair. This section describes the motivation behind the construction of each of the four citadels.

"Citadel" came into the English language around 1500 from the Italian *citadella*. Rulers of the Italian city states constructed forts, as much to keep their citizens in awe and subjection as to defend them. An early English reference speaks of citadels as "nests of tyranny." Initially, *citadellas*, or little cities, were independent of a city's main defences. By the 17th century, citadels became embedded into a city's walls so that these two means of defence could sup-

port each other. They became immensely strong forts of four or five bastions with garrisons of 4000 or more.

French military engineer Sebastien Le Prestre de Vauban incorporated citadels into a number of forts he constructed in the last half of the 17th century. Although complex in execution, Vauban's principles can be readily understood as applied to the four citadels erected in Halifax, which were small in scale compared to the massive fortifications he built surrounding the city of Strasbourg or those for Neuf-Brisach in Alsace-Lorraine.

In the last decades of the 19th century, rapid changes in armaments made the Citadel obsolete, but it continued to serve as a headquarters and barracks for a small British garrison until its withdrawal in 1906. The Citadel's role in guarding the port of Halifax was negligible, but it was not abandoned and was put to use during both world wars. It remained part of the defence infrastructure until 1951 when it was transferred into civilian hands and became the historic site we see today.

Map showing the town plan of Halifax

Chapter 4

A City Founded and
a Citadel Erected

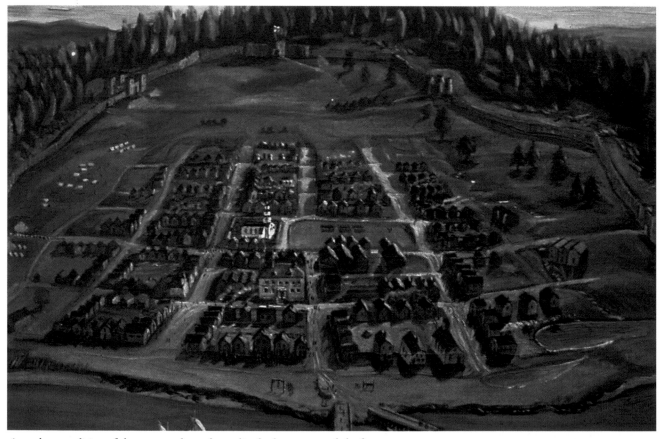

A modern rendition of the town and wooden palisade that connected the forts

In 1713, during a period of peace after one of the many Anglo-French wars for North American supremacy, Britain gained control of mainland Nova Scotia.

Nevertheless, the British made no attempt to settle the colony. Other than maintaining a pitiful garrison at Annapolis Royal, they did nothing to counter the massive

French fort at Louisbourg, being built according to Vauban's theories. Then came the War of the Austrian Succession and Louisbourg's startling capture by New England forces in 1745. By the 1748 Treaty of Aix-la-Chapelle Britain restored Louisbourg to France, but the war had demonstrated the military importance of establishing a counterweight to Louisbourg. More significantly, the British recognized that English settlement was now a necessity to make Nova Scotia truly a British colony and to create a strategic buffer for New England.

On June 26, 1749, with a commission as Captain General and Governor of Nova Scotia, Colonel the Honourable Edward Cornwallis arrived at Chebucto Bay aboard the *Sphinx*, soon to be joined by 2,576 settlers. After examining possible sites for the town, to be named Halifax in honour of the Earl of Halifax, President of the Board of Trade and Plantations, Cornwallis selected an area on the west side of the harbour narrows:

Edward Cornwallis,
founder of Halifax

> *upon the side of a hill which commands the whole peninsula and shelters the town from the north-west winds. From the shore to the top of the hill is about half a mile, the ascent very gentle, the soil is good, there is a convenient landing for the boats along the beach and good anchorage within gunshot of the shore for the largest ships.*

When Cornwallis's military engineer, John Brewse, prepared a plan for the immediate defence of the fledgling town, it called for five stockaded forts or wooden blockhouses, to be linked by lines of wooden palisades on the town's perimeter. The first fort was erected below the summit, on the south side of the hill, overlooking the town and harbour. Brewse named this fort the Citadel.

By September the Citadel was completed. It was square with sides measuring 125 feet and had a bastion at each corner. In its construction, double rows of pickets were used, with the second row filling in the hollows where the front row pickets touched each other. Musket loopholes were cut. By using bastions, the forts could be integrated into the wooden palisade, which was completed in the following year. Musket fire from the bastions could not only cover adjoining bastions and connecting walls or curtains, but also swept along across the lines of palisades. Inside the fort was accommodation for 100 men. These forts and palisades served to protect the Halifax town proper from minor raids.

Although Britain and France were officially at peace, both sides prepared for the next round in the struggle for North America. Cornwallis fortified George's Island in the summer of 1750 to cover the immediate harbour approaches in front of the town. He deployed sixteen 24- and 32-pounders, powerful cannon for their day. Then he had a battery erected on the Dartmouth side to cover the eastern passage into the harbour. Three more batteries were built on the Halifax side with a total of 44 guns. Other than a full-scale French sea borne invasion, Halifax's defences could protect the town, and especially the naval establishment.

War broke out unofficially in 1755 when the British captured Fort Beauséjour on the Chignecto Isthmus. All threat to Halifax was removed when the British forces used the town as a base to capture Louisbourg in 1758. Under General James Wolfe, the British went on to take Quebec in the next year.

With the struggle for North America over and peace in 1763, the Citadel blockhouse and other forts fell into decay. Military recognition, however, that in order to defend Halifax the hill had to be the "principal Object of Attention" because it was so high above the surrounding ground, meant that "whoever is Master of it is so of the whole." Military engineers proposed a five-sided fort with detached bastions projecting towards the town. But they also recognized that the summit was so narrow that no substantial fort could be built without considerable cutting down of the hill.

In 1761, Major General John Henry Bastide, who had been a military engineer at both Louisbourg sieges, prepared a report on Halifax defences that brought to the fore the question of strategic purpose and type of future fortifications. For Bastide, Halifax was best suited in North America, particularly because of its harbour and location, to serve the army and navy as a base in war and in peace to check an enemy's aggressive designs, but also to serve as a "weight" to keep the colonies "in proper subordination." Bastide concluded that a citadel on the most commanding ground, enclosed with bastions and curtains, would be the best method of defence from landward attack.

Although a fort was never built according to his plan, the hill was cut down 40 feet in 1761.

The American Revolution and a Second Citadel

After the Battle of Lexington between British troops and Massachusetts's colonials on April 18, 1775, a colonial army besieged British troops in Boston. Halifax then became the only secure base for desperately need supplies. As Nova Scotia's governor, Francis Legge, explained to his superiors in London, Halifax was the single port left with a Royal Dockyard where ships could be cleaned and have a supply of masts, and to where troops could retreat if necessary. There was not the least kind of defence about the town, he reported; the batteries were

The second citadel, built in the 1770s, was a maze of earthworks overlooked by a blockhouse, as shown in this modern painting

all dismantled with their gun carriages decayed and lying on the ground. Only 36 troops remained in the town and no vessels were assigned to the station. During that summer of 1775, Halifax, completely open to attack, was a strategic prize that taken would have made Britain's position untenable. It would have secured to the Americans, at a stroke, one of the two bases left in British hands for mounting operations against the revolting colonies. Instead, the Americans chose to invade Canada, only to face complete defeat before the walls of Quebec.

General Thomas Gage, leader of the besieged troops in Boston, advised that the militia begin building temporary defences, though it proved too late in the season for work to be commenced even on Citadel Hill itself. But the critical time for Halifax and its population of 5000 had, fortunately, passed. In the early spring of 1776, on the decision to evacuate Boston, 11,000 soldiers and 1100 Loyalists arrived in Halifax.

As part of the plan to defend Nova Scotia, what was left of the bastioned fortification was demolished and a new work erected. The planned fort was fairly substantial, but became a maze-like system of rambling ill-planned multi-sided earthworks, erratically running down the hill's slopes. A contemporary commented that the earthwork "rose in Amphitheatre one above the other, twisting around the Hill in different Shapes and Levels" with the hill's crown more exposed than any other part. Within it, cannon were mounted to cover the naval yard and the open country towards the North West Arm. Two large powder magazines were constructed and wells dug to ensure a water supply.

Although American privateers pillaged Lunenburg and other parts of the province, Halifax was not threatened for the

Sir John Wentworth, Governor of Nova Scotia (Robert Field)

remainder of the war. In July 1783 Lieutenant Colonel Robert Morse, as Chief Engineer in North America, arrived in Halifax with orders to report on future defences for Nova Scotia. He found "Citadel Hill... one of the most unexceptionable [sic] situations for a fortress I ever saw." A respectable fort erected on it with casemated barracks for 600 to 800 men, he believed, would force an attacker to undertake a siege on unfavourable ground. He went as far as to recommend that the whole of Halifax's defences should be concentrated on a single substantial fort with the outer and supporting forts abandoned. Probably realizing that such a recommendation would not be followed because of the coming of peace, he allowed himself the comment that "it is in time of peace we should guard against war."

As with the first citadel, the earthworks were allowed to decay until they became totally useless. When military authorities decided to remove the blockhouse in 1789 because it was in such a ruinous condition, they assured Halifax merchants that the flag and signal staff would remain.

Prince Edward and a Third Citadel

When Halifax first learned in April 1793 that war with revolutionary France had broken out, the Citadel was a hopeless ruin and other defences no better. Even the gun platforms had been allowed to rot beyond use. From London came orders to dispatch to the West Indies all but 200 of the garrison with a single frigate left for naval defence. Governor John Wentworth was told to raise a provincial regiment and make the militia ready to repel a French attack.

In the United States a former French diplomat turned fiery revolutionist, Edmund Genêt, was campaigning for American support. A French fleet arrived in New York to refit. Genêt proposed using it to destroy the British fishing fleet off Newfoundland and to burn Halifax. In October, Wentworth received intelligence that the fleet was making ready to sail. Fearing an immediate attack, Wentworth ordered the militia from the counties to march to Halifax with all speed. While the militia and regulars could have repulsed any attempted landing, the French fleet could have bombarded and fired the town with virtual impunity. Fortunately for Halifax the crews mutinied, and the admiral of the fleet, after quarrelling with Genêt, sailed for France. At no time had Halifax been more threatened and its defences more ill-prepared to resist such a sea borne attack.

This changed dramatically when Prince Edward, fourth son of George III, came to Halifax as commander of the troops in Nova Scotia and New Brunswick. Early in life Edward had lost the favour of his father, who had sent him to military schools in Germany and Switzerland; the King was determined to keep Edward out of England. In 1791, as commanding officer of his regiment the 7th Foot, Edward took up station in Quebec. When war broke out, he seized the opportunity to see active service, which he did as a brigade commander in the capture of two West Indian islands, St. Lucia and Martinique.

Aged 27, Edward arrived in Halifax on June 28, 1794 to take up his command.

Mme. de St. Laurent (above), companion to Prince Edward, Duke of Kent (below)

Accompanying him was Thérèse-Bernardine Mongenet, known as Mme de Saint-Laurent. He was devoted to her and only in 1818, when there was danger of failure in the royal succession, did he give up his Julie, as he called her, marry a widow of a German prince and go on to father Queen Victoria.

As a royal prince, Edward felt free to draw on the British treasury for large sums; he used that freedom to put Halifax in a state of defence against any further French attacks. Starting in 1795, spending soared; in that year Edward drew on the treasury for £100,000, and he continued to draw for such amounts until he had transformed Halifax's defences into an array of fortifications to protect the town and its seaward approaches.

Edward began with Citadel Hill. He and his chief engineer, Captain James Straton, agreed that money spent on repair would be folly. What was required was a more simple and compact design, conforming better to the ground than its predecessor, while providing greater defence against attack from the landward side of the hill. The natural approach to attack Halifax was to sail up the North West Arm and land the forces to mount a siege from the west. Less than 700 yards to the southwest of Citadel Hill lay high ground, known as Camp Hill, where an attacker could place siege batteries.

Straton began by confronting the chief obstacle to fortifying Citadel Hill: its summit, so dominant when seen from the harbour, was, in fact, an attenuated egg-shaped ridge running on a northwest-southeast

20th-century artist's impression of Fort George, the third citadel

line. Its sheer narrowness made it impossible to superimpose a Vauban star-shaped fort, without massively cutting down the hill. As a drumlin (a geographical feature resulting from glacial drift) having no bedrock, the hill could be cut down to whatever level desired. But, if cut down to an ideal level, the hill would no longer dominate Camp Hill to the west. Straton decided first to level the site where the old Citadel stood and then cut 14 feet off the summit. His plan called for an elongated, symmetrical earthwork with four bastions, conforming to the ground, but resulting in the east and west sides being more than double the length of those on the north and south.

With a steep slope on the harbour side running all the way down to the water's edge, some 700 yards, Straton felt confident any infantry attack from that direction could be defeated.

Attacking ships in the harbour battering his citadel would have to do so from 1000 yards and at a 10-degree angle of elevation, making any such bombardment likely ineffective.

The west side was most vulnerable to landward attack. He planned for the bastions on this western front to be much larger than those on the eastern, making the western curtain much shorter. Although the faces of the western bastions could be defended from the flanks of their adjacent bastions, much ground remained not covered by fire. Within the citadel, a large cavalier barracks for 650 men was made of heavy timber and made bomb-proof by being heavily banked on top with earth. Twenty 24-pounder cannon were mounted on its roof, half directed west and half east. To this third fort on Citadel Hill, Prince Edward gave the name Fort George, in honour of his father, the King.

Early 20th-century view from Citadel Hill, with George's Island and the harbour mouth in the background.

With attack up the North West Arm still a concern, Prince Edward had a battery built near its entrance and behind it a Martello tower (a round ironstone fort, today a National Historic Site). Its walls measured eight feet at the base and six feet at the top, with cannon mounted on its top and space for a 100-man garrison. Prince Edward named it the Prince of Wales Tower after his brother, who would become George IV.

All these fortifications required labour drawn from the 7th Foot and the enrolled militia, as well as civilian workers engaged for the construction season. As many as 300 to 400 workers were recruited for the Citadel, but war had created a severe labour shortage. Prince Edward seized the opportunity to recruit as many Maroons as he could, immediately on their arrival from Jamaica in July 1796.

Maroons were descended from renegade slaves who had fled to Jamaica's hilly interior after the British conquest in 1665. Proud, of magnificent physique, warlike and fiercely indepen-

Although the third citadel was built mostly of wood, in this modern painting the Maroons are shown building a section of masonry wall.

dent, they had created communities in the hills from which they fought an on-and-off guerrilla war with the whites. After an unsuccessful revolt, 650 Maroons were sent to Halifax, with the expectation that they would proceed to Sierra Leone, though this did not happen until the summer of 1800. Those Maroons Prince Edward recruited constructed one of the bastions, which became called the "Maroon Bastion."

Prince Edward undertook the construction or improvement of such other works as a star-shaped fort on Georges Island named Fort Charlotte after the Queen, York Redoubt off the

peninsula covering the entrances to Halifax Harbour and the North West Arm and Fort Clarence on the Dartmouth side of the harbour. To provide warning of attack and to communicate with the outer forts, he established a visual telegraph system.

Prince Edward's system consisted of wooden towers, supporting flagstaffs and yardarms for sending messages by flags and balls. Towers were situated so that messages could be read using telescopes. Initially, the system served as a means of communication with the outer forts, with the Citadel, where the tower was located on the Cavalier Barracks, its

Leonard Parkinson, a captain of the Maroons

house a garrison clock; two years later he sent instructions to London for the purchase of clock works. When, however, Governor Sir John Wentworth found that the clock's site was to be away from the town on the south side of Citadel Hill, he roused the merchant community to raise sufficient funds to pay for a building upon which to place the clock. A key condition was for the clock to be built on the east glacis (its present location), so it could be readily seen by the townspeople, who now numbered 9,000.

Responsibility for designing and constructing the tower for housing the clock remained with the military. Of clearly classical composition, the tower is a three-tiered irregular octagon, with its wooden facade handled like stone, and atop a rectangular building with simple doric columns at each corner. Although greatly overshadowed in scale by such other Halifax examples of Georgian classicism as St. George's, the Round Church (also built of wood) or the imposing sandstone edifices of Government House and Province House, the clock's architectural symmetry, balance and simplicity of ornament have made it Halifax's most enduring and endearing landmark.

British naval supremacy provided Halifax and British North America with all the protection they required against French attack. But deteriorating Anglo-American relations over the use of this naval supremacy to intercept neutral shipping in the struggle with Napoleon threatened hostilities. If war should come, then British strategy would be based on defending Quebec and Halifax, the two most vital positions for preserving British North America. The American seizure of Halifax, the British government in a secret instruction informed Sir James Craig, governor in chief at Quebec, would mean the loss of the "most important Naval Station in the North American continent." War did come in 1812, but New England neutrality and American naval weakness allowed Nova Scotia to benefit enormously from privateering and extensive smuggling, while remaining free from any threat of attack. It was said during this war that the streets of Halifax were paved with gold.

With Napoleon's abdication and exile to Elba in early 1814, British military and naval forces were freed to enter the war against the Americans. The whole eastern American seaboard lay under a tightening blockade, while the British

nerve centre. From his residence overlooking Bedford Basin, Edward could communicate within minutes to all the forts. Later, he expanded it to Windsor and Annapolis Royal; messages could be sent to Windsor some 40 miles away, for example, in 20 minutes. Prince Edward intended his telegraph to reach Quebec, but cost and manpower demands precluded it.

As early as 1761, the Nova Scotia House of Assembly had voted £50 for a town clock, but nothing came of this until around 1800 when Prince Edward ordered the Royal Engineers Department to prepare plans for a building to

Late 19th-century view of Halifax harbour from the Citadel with garrison soldiers in the foreground

mounted sea borne operations against Washington, which they burned in retaliation for the American burning of York (Toronto), and New Orleans. From Halifax in September the British mounted an operation that with little resistance occupied most of eastern Maine. Massive smuggling, heartily endorsed by the British, began with merchants on both sides exchanging American agricultural produce and timber for manufactured goods from England. Those Americans who took an oath of allegiance to George III were accorded the same commercial privileges as British subjects. A good number did so. All came to an end with the signing of the peace Treaty of Ghent on Christmas Eve 1814, though it was not proclaimed in Halifax until March 1815.

News of Wellington's defeat of Napoleon at Waterloo reached Halifax on July 19, 1815. At the Mason's Hall, Attorney General Richard John Uniacke chaired a celebration dinner. With 101 toasts to be drunk, the dinner went on into the morning. A friend of Uniacke's met the tall, powerful Irishman in the street and enquired if the dinner was over. "Not at all," roared Uniacke in laughter, "I'm away home for my snuffbox and then back to finish the toasts." Such was Halifax's mood as it entered a century of peace. On Citadel Hill, the earthwork was left to the rain and the frost until there was nothing left but "a heap of ruins."

Chapter 5

THE FOURTH CITADEL

For the defence of the Canadas (Ontario and Quebec) the chief strategic lesson learned from the War of 1812 was the critical importance of naval control of the Great Lakes. Yet, the costs for Britain to maintain a permanent naval establishment in peacetime were prohibitive. As well, such a presence would serve as an irritant at a time when British policy sought to improve Anglo-American relations. With the signing of the Rush-Bagot agreement in 1817 to demilitarize the Great Lakes, the strategy for the defence of British North America had to be re-thought. There remained much suspicion and hostility, and British strategic planning continued to assume the likelihood of another war. During the 19th century there were a number of Anglo-American disputes that could have led to war, particularly after the American Civil War began.

After the Duke of Wellington became Master General of Ordnance and responsible for British imperial fortifications, he advocated a defensive strategy for British North America, emphasizing strong fortifications and improved communications between the Atlantic and the interior. In his instructions to a commission of three engineering officers sent to British North America in 1825 to report on a system of defence, Wellington directed that they examine the ground on which the Citadel in Halifax stood with a view either to its repair or the construction of a larger fort, for the defence of the harbour, and to be garrisoned by 200 or 300 men.

The Smyth Commission, as it became called, recommended the construction of permanent masonry forts at Montreal, Quebec, Kingston, Niagara and Halifax. Although on land a defensive strategy was all that would be possible, it suggested seaborne attacks, as launched during the War of 1812 against Washington and Maine, could be once more undertaken against such cities as New York.

For Halifax, with the enemy at the door, the commission believed

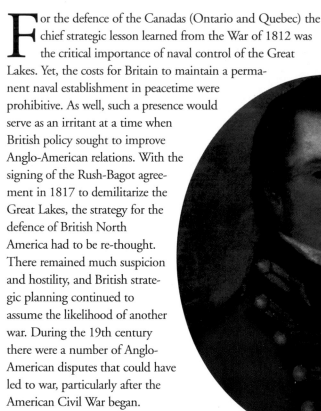

Colonel Gustavus Nicolls R.E., who was responsible for the plan of the fourth citadel

Modern impression of construction activity on the fourth citadel

it became more urgent and indispensable to erect a fort on Citadel Hill to give protection to the town and support for the sea batteries. It envisioned an assault on the harbour defences or a landing at a nearby location and attack from the rear. A strongly fortified Citadel Hill would give confidence to the troops and militia employed to meet such an attacking force.

Colonel Gustavus Nicolls, Commander of the Royal Engineers in Halifax, supported the commission's recommendations, adding in his view:

> the good effect it would have on the Morale of the natives, as well as the contrary on that of their neighbours the Americans, who when on their frequent visits to this harbour, see its shores bristling with cannon on every side,

and the British flag flying on the Citadel...are thoroughly deterred from making an attack on Halifax.

Designing and Constructing the Citadel

Nicolls drew the plans for a four-bastioned citadel of permanent building materials. Although the eastern and western fronts were still twice the length of those on the north and south, the additional space allowed for ravelins on each of these fronts and also on the west front to provide the ramparts with greater protection. The shortness of the north and south fronts made the use of three-sided demi-bastions necessary. Masonry construction, however, allowed Nicolls to incorporate not only casemates (vaulted bomb-proofed

Artillerymen at the Citadel entrance, c. 1885.

chambers for barracks and cannon) in cavaliers and the ramparts, but also to construct a counterscarp with a musketry gallery running round the citadel's perimeter.

Approval of Nicolls's plans arrived in 1828, in time to commence digging the ditch in front of the western ravelin, the lowest section of the western front. Both civilian contractors and members of the Royal Sappers and Miners sent out from England worked on the Citadel. Tens of thousands of choice squared, quarry-faced ironstone blocks were brought by vessel from the King's Quarries on the west side of the North West Arm. Probably the busiest construction season proved to be that of 1830 when as many as 350 men were at work. Of these, nearly 200 were civilian labourers, masons and carpenters. Around 30 loads of stone a day were being hauled up the hill. Numerous horse-drawn carts, filled with

lime, sand, timber and other supplies, also found ready employment.

Also in 1830, work began on the two-storey Cavalier Barracks, each storey having seven casemates and topped by a roof of heavy timbers and earth capable of supporting seven 24-pounder guns on traversing platforms. The wall on the more threatened western side was six feet deep, but half that thickness on the eastern. For its front, Nicolls designed a two-storey colonnaded veranda open at each end; later it was closed in with stairs at each end as it is reconstructed today. Even later, when all thought was given up of putting cannon on the roof, a wooden third storey with a gable roof was added.

Nicolls came under pressure to reduce mounting costs. One solution, which had the advantage of increasing barrack space through the use of additional casemates, was to replace the planned ravelin on the east side with a large redan. A wide angled "V" projection extending outwards, the redan was fully part of the east front's ramparts and incorporated the Citadel's main entrance, unlike the ravelins on the other fronts, which were detached outer works.

Nicolls, also to save expense, made the specifications at the base and top for the retaining walls on the northwest and southwest bastions far too narrow. As a result, these walls could not withstand the effects of the freeze-thaw cycle which caused the earth in the ramparts between the two walls to expand. As Nicolls ruefully remarked in a personal letter, he had "made a little too free with the climate." Nicolls was ordered to rebuild the walls to the mean thickness, as laid down by Vauban, whose dimensions had the "advantage of long experience."

In the 1840s two bomb-proof magazines were constructed in the northwest and southwest demi-bastions. Built of granite, they had a combined capacity of nearly 4000 barrels of gunpowder.

For a garrison of up to 1000 men, and the possibility of a long siege, a safe and sufficient water supply and drainage system was critical. As well, there had to be separate drainage for the ditch to keep it dry and thus reduce possible frost damage to the stone walls. Three large rain-water tanks and part of a complicated system of pipes to collect and store surface water were placed beneath the parade square on the east side. In addition, there were two wells, one of which was probably the oldest in Halifax, dating from the second Citadel, and then 106 feet deep, but later deepened to 160 feet.

No aspect of the Citadel has aroused greater curiosity than the tradition of a mysterious and secret tunnel from the Citadel to George's Island. What does exist is a large and well-constructed brick sewer, which is high enough for a man, albeit stooping, to walk its course. From the Citadel it runs down the glacis, connects with a large stone drain (on the site of an ancient stream), and thence down to the harbour.

Beneath the ramparts are the six sally ports constructed around 1836 to allow troops to pass through the ramparts and down to and across the ditch to reach the counterscarp with its loop-holed musketry galleries and chambers. They also allowed for access to the bomb-proof guard houses in the north, south and west ravelins.

In the Citadel's construction nothing bedeviled its builders more than the changing numbers and types of casemates, and especially the challenge of making them waterproof. In all, the Citadel has 80 arched structures that can be loosely defined as casemates, used for such varied purposes as barracks, officer quarters, privies, storage, prison cells, kitchens and for mounting cannon.

For Citadel engineers, the most daunting challenge was finding a satisfactory covering and drainage system that would ensure the casemates remained dry in the Halifax winter with its sudden thaws. Although all casemates were constructed by 1848, though no complete satisfactory answer was ever found. A primary solution proved to be the extensive use of the newly patented product called asphalt. With the casemates finally habitable, the Citadel could be fully garrisoned. Officers and men of the 76th Foot had the honour of being the first garrison for the Citadel when they moved into quarters during the spring of 1856. To withstand a six-week siege it was estimated that a garrison would need 900 infantry, 340 artillerymen and 120 sappers.

By 1856, after 28 years of construction, it could be said the Halifax Citadel was operational at a cost of £242,122, somewhat above its original estimate of £116,000.

Arming the Citadel

Arming the Citadel had begun the previous decade with the 1848 arrival of a vessel-load of 32-pounder cannon manufactured at the Royal Arsenal at Woolwich on the Thames River, near London. On this event the *Morning Courier* commented that "This important fortress is rapidly assuming all the characteristics of its name and when completed will be the lion of, and is already the centre of attraction to the numerous visitors that weekly walk around its frowning battlements." In 1853 the *Novascotian* noted that the Citadel was fast being equipped with cannon of very heavy calibre — 8-inch shell guns. By 1856 the Citadel's armament consisted of twenty 24-pounders to put in defence casemates to cover the ditch, forty-five 32-pounders for the ramparts and ravelins and to be placed on the Cavalier Barracks. In addition, five of the 8-inch shell guns, the largest (10 feet 3 inches in length) and heaviest (65 hundred weight) of this weapon class were mounted at the five corners. Considered the most suitable for coastal defence, it was designed to fire spherical shells up to 3000 yards. Although it could fire different shell types, the most common was fixed shrapnel, containing 339 one-ounce bullets. There was a single 12-pounder signal gun, which was likely mounted on the ramparts, though it may have been on the east glacis.

Halifax Merchants and the Signal Station

As noted earlier, Prince Edward had a signal station erected on the Citadel for a visual telegraph system. It communicated through two intervening stations with the harbour approaches at Sambro. A signal, using flags and disks, would indicate military intelligence about vessels entering the harbour. The tall signal mast on the Citadel was used for this purpose.

The commercial mast — the shorter of the two — would carry flags on merchant shipping. For example, a red flag for a ship from Europe, blue for one from the West Indies. Halifax merchants soon saw the commercial advantages of this system and each firm had its private signals, which could be flown from the commercial mast when one of its vessels was approaching.

During construction of the new Citadel, Nicolls placed the tall signal mast and military telegraph mast on the ramparts of the southeastern front, while the flag pole for the Union Jack was put on the southwest demi-bastion. By the mid-1850s some 2,000 vessels were annually entering the harbour. Merchants and employees would watch the commercial mast with great anticipation. On sighting their private signal floating in the wind, there would be much scurrying on the wharves to be on hand when the vessel arrived.

The system was of increasing commercial importance after Samuel Cunard, a Halifax merchant and founder of Cunard Steamships, inaugurated in 1840 regular transatlantic steamship service for mail and passengers. As the signal system on Citadel Hill gave notice some hours before the Royal Mail Steamers' arrival, mails to and from Europe and the Unites States could be made up and ships not detained longer than necessary. With the development of the electric telegraph, the military, however, had no further use for the system and was no longer prepared to bear the costs, much to the merchants' consternation. Such was the concern that the Nova Scotia government agreed in 1858 to defray the expense of the military continuing to operate the system by charging a fee to all vessels entering the port.

A Formidable Challenge

On its completion, the Halifax Citadel became the strongest bastion for the defence of British North America in an Anglo-American war. For any American attack to be successful, it had to result in the capture of the naval station, which was critical to Britain's ability to reinforce inland garrisons and above all, to use its sea power to advantage. In the 1850s British naval supremacy remained unchallenged. For American warships to penetrate the inner harbour and destroy the naval station and dockyard, they had to fight their way past outer batteries on the harbour approaches and then take on the Citadel. With wooden warships, notoriously ineffective against masonry fortifications, such an attack had virtually no chance of success.

Any successful attack on Halifax therefore had to include the landing of a sufficient force that could first overcome resistance to the landing and lay siege to the Citadel. Even if the attackers destroyed the naval station and dockyard, unless they captured the Citadel their position would rapidly become untenable. The only ground that lent itself to siege operations was Camp Hill, which provided sufficient cover to establish a siege camp, but faced the Citadel's strongly defended western front.

A siege against such a strong fortification as the Citadel would have involved digging an advancing series of zigzag approach and parallel supporting trenches to reach the top of the glacis overlooking the ditch. Although sandbagging and bundles of long sticks — fascines — provided some protection, this would have been arduous and dangerous work done under constant fire from the guns on the west ravelin and the northwest and southwest demi-bastions. Once the parallels had reached near enough, the attacker would have established siege batteries that could engage and destroy the guns and their crews on the ramparts and concentrate fire on the wall where the breach was to be made. Mining and explosives could also be used to make the breach. Capturing the west

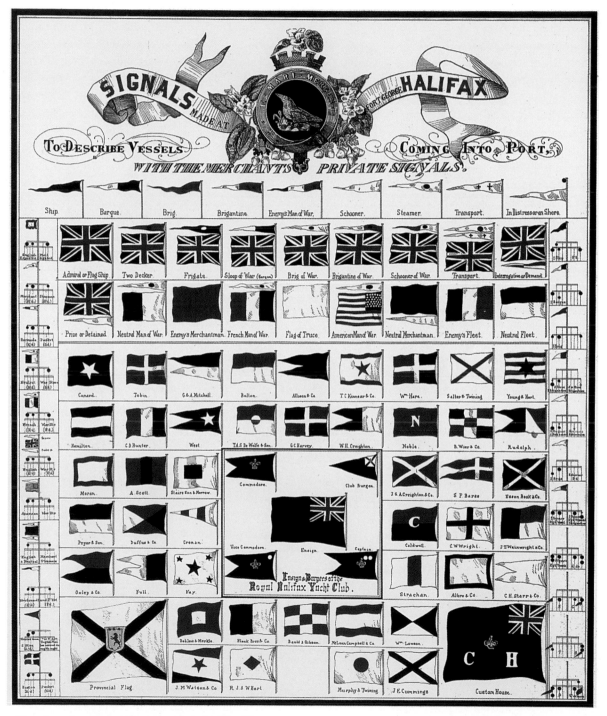

Signals used on the masts mounted at the Citadel

ravelin would have been necessary before any assault could have been made on the main walls and so it would have been the first point of attack.

The final assault required sending infantry storming parties into the ditch to capture the wall area that had been breached or use ladders to mount the ramparts. Storming parties could suffer dreadful casualties as the British army experienced in its failed assaults during the Crimean War to capture the Russian naval base of Sebastopol in an 11-month siege. Never attacked, the Halifax Citadel by its formidable presence served to guard Halifax and the British North American colonies as they grew into the nation Canada.

Canada Takes Over the Citadel

In the early 1880s significant technological advances permitted the manufacture of breech-loading artillery and naval guns that could fire further and faster than rifled muzzle loaders, which soon became obsolete. To deal with naval ships bombarding Halifax and its dockyard from miles offshore, between 1885 and 1905 some £838,000 was spent in improving old fortifications or constructing new ones, and mounting breech loaders at the harbour's outer reaches. One of the Royal Artillery officers responsible for this rearmament was Captain Frederick James Odevaine, grandfather of this writer. While in Halifax he married Mildred Uniacke Cady, but tragically drowned while skating at Williams Lake.

The accelerating technological changes in armaments posed major dilemmas for imperial defence. None more so than for

Captain Frederick James Odevaine, responsible for rearmament of the Citadel

the Royal Navy as navies of rival imperial powers rapidly grew in size and armament, while ship construction costs soared. No longer could Britain maintain naval supremacy the world over. At the same time, the growing power of Imperial Germany caused Britain to abandon its policy of "Splendid Isolation" and to enter into an *Entente Cordiale* with France and Russia. It also meant the end of Royal Naval squadrons stationed around the world in the cause of imperial defence, to be replaced by a home-based navy equipped with *Dreadnoughts*, the world's first "all-big-gun" warship.

The Garrison Goes Home

Although after Confederation Britain continued in its commitment to defend the new Dominion, it sought also, increasingly, to transfer responsibility to Canada for its own defence. Britain withdrew all its forces from North America except for the Halifax garrison in 1871, though later there would be a small garrison at the Esquimalt naval station on Vancouver Island. With Malta, Gibraltar and Bermuda, Halifax remained a key station for imperial defence and went through two major rearmaments, first with rifled muzzle loaders and then with breech loaders. But as the needs for British home defence grew, the Halifax garrison was reduced to a single infantry battalion in 1884. Then, in 1900, the demands of the Boer War saw the remaining battalion leave and be replaced by the 5th Battalion, the Royal Garrison Regiment. It was made up of officers and men who had retired from active service, but re-engaged for garrison duty. Garrison battalions proved both expensive and of doubtful military capability.

Great Britain's determination to withdraw its remaining forces from Canada came at a time when rising Canadian nationalism and fervent imperial loyalty came together to shape national policy. As a self-governing Dominion within the British Empire, Canada had answered the imperial call to fight in the South African war and it now accepted responsibility for Halifax's defences and naval dockyard. On January 16, 1906, the official transfer to Canadian control took place after 157 years of British military presence in Halifax. Six companies of the Royal Canadian Regiment with the Royal Canadian Garrison Artillery now manned the forts with the Citadel continuing to serve as a barracks and headquarters. An editorial in the Halifax *Morning Chronicle*, aptly entitled "Another National and Imperial Step," greeted with "sincere and unalloyed pleasure" the transfer so conducive to "complete Canadian nationhood" and "British [Imperial] Federation," while assuring uneasy merchants and shopkeepers that there was not likely "to be any diminution in military expenditures here."

The Citadel in World War One

Although kept secret at the time of the transfer, if Canada had not taken over responsibility for Halifax, British policy was to leave it defenceless as the prevailing view held that Halifax would "be of little strategical importance" in a European war. When war came in August 1914, however,

Mildred Uniacke Cady met and married Capt. Odevaine while he was stationed in Halifax

Halifax became of critical importance for the assembly and defence of convoys, the lifeline across the Atlantic and the dispatch overseas of 400,000 Canadian troops.

As well as serving as a command headquarters and barracks, from 1914 to 1916 German prisoners of war were kept in the Citadel. With all the normal military activities continuing within the Citadel, it proved difficult to ensure proper security. In one case prisoners in the northeast salient used a table knife to saw through a bar in a casemate. With a ladder fashioned from a rope and coat hangers, they dropped into the ditch and climbed the counterscarp. They were recaptured, but later all prisoners were sent to an internment camp at Amherst. Although commonly believed that Leon Trotsky, the Russian revolutionary, was interned in the Citadel in April 1917, this was not the case. Halifax authorities did take Trotsky off a ship from New York en route to Russia, but sent him to Amherst for internment. After the new Russian government, which had replaced the overthrown Tsar, successfully requested his release, Trotsky left Halifax to make revolutionary history.

Restoration Projects to Save the Citadel

In December 1931 the Royal Canadian Regiment marched out of the Citadel for the last time. As the military had no further use for it, there was talk of Halifax taking it over with some suggesting the hill should be levelled and the site used for housing. Nothing came of the idea with the deepening

Entrance to Citadel, Halifax, N.S.

Great Depression. By the winter of 1932, an estimated 3,000 men were on relief in Halifax. On the city's initiative, an Unemployment Relief Project was authorized in which 300 World War One veterans on relief were to be housed and fed in the Citadel and put to work restoring the walls. As well, accommodation in casemates, cookhouses, mess halls and laundry facilities were established. A canteen provided magazines, newspapers and had a gramophone donated by Halifax citizens. The men were paid 20 cents for an eight-hour day.

A priority of the work project was the construction of a driveway around the Citadel with a new access road from North Park Street. This was completed fairly quickly. Work then began on dismantling the most dangerous walls, leaving reconstruction to later. A light railway was built to handle the granite blocks, which weighed between 500 and 850 pounds apiece. By the end of the project in 1936, considerable work had been done, but left were thousands of tons of stone litter-ing the ditch and parade square.

If it achieved little else, the Relief Project had focused attention on preserving the Citadel because it was such a summer tourist attraction. In 1936 it attracted 5000 visitors. Public pressure brought a grant from the federal government to clean up the debris left by the Relief Project and to repair access roads. With the Second World War the military re-occupied the Citadel.

Citadel Preserved

After the war the Department of National Defence entered into negotiations for the Citadel's transfer to Halifax or another government department as a means of preserving it. Back in 1935 the Historic Sites and Monuments Board had officially recognized the Citadel as structure of national historic importance. When the Royal Commission on National Development in the Arts, Letters and Sciences (the Massey Commission) visited in 1950, it found progressive deterioration and urged action. A year later National Defence transferred the Citadel to Resources and Development, the department responsible for heritage preservation. Initially, the Citadel became a repository for historical displays in association with such private and provincial museums as the Army and Navy Museums and an annex of the Nova Scotia Museum of Science. It continued to be a major draw for tourists.

As important as preserving the Citadel as an historic structure was preserving views from Citadel Hill overlooking the harbour. During the 1960s higher and higher buildings began to appear in Halifax's downtown business district. When opposition developed to proposals for towers that would block views from the hill, the lines were drawn in what became known as "The Battle of Citadel Hill." It pitted heritage and other citizens' groups against those who believed that Halifax's need for development should override any heritage concerns. In 1974 city council passed a View Planes By-law; a compromise, but one that has stood the test of time and gained virtual complete public acceptance.

The Citadel as a National Historic Site

In 1951 the National Historic Sites and Monuments Board declared the Halifax Citadel to be a National Historic Site. This declaration eventually led to a major research and restoration programme involving many historical researchers, architects and archaeologists. Over the next

One o'clock Gun, Halifax, N.S.

Guns were fired daily from the Citadel at various times during the course of its history

In the high season, from Victoria Day in May to Thanksgiving in October, Halifax Citadel comes alive with the sounds of pipers and drummers, drilling 78th Highlanders and Royal Artillery gun crews demonstrating their skills. Historical restoration and interpretation at the Citadel are neverending tasks. They have as their overriding challenge to bring to life a fort and its garrison in a city whose story in our nation's history stretches back over 250 years.

(Above and below) Reconstruction project on the Citadel walls gave work to World War One veterans

three decades much work had to be done to reconstruct and restore walls and buildings. For purposes of thematic interpretation, the period 1869-71 was chosen because, with the mounting of rifled muzzle loaders as its main armament, the Citadel was at its peak effectiveness against attack from sea or from land. These were the years when the 78th Highlanders were in garrison and so this regiment has become the focus of interpretation.

ACKNOWLEDGEMENTS

In writing this book I have had the benefit of numerous research publications, most written by Parks Canada historians. Harry Piers' *The Evolution of Halifax Fortress 1749-1928* and published by the Public Archives of Nova Scotia in 1947 remains essential, along with John Joseph Greenough's *The Halifax Citadel, 1825-60: A Narrative and Structural History*; a Parks Canada publication of 1977, for the Citadel's construction history. On the social and regimental history relating to the Citadel, Cameron Pulsifer's research reports for Parks Canada, in particular his "The 78th Highlanders in Halifax, 1869-71: The Experiences of a Highland Regiment in a Garrison Town" proved most useful. As did Clarence MacKinnon's 1965 doctoral thesis for the University of Toronto "The Imperial Fortresses of Canada: Halifax and Esquimalt 1871-1906." I also relied upon Brenda Dunn's "The Halifax Citadel, 1906-51: The Canadian Period" and Barbara Schmeisser, "Town Clock 1803-1860: A Structural and Narrative Study," both of which are Parks Canada Manuscript Reports.

I wish to extend my thanks to Dr. R.H. McDonald and the Parks Canada staff at the Halifax Citadel for their assistance and especially that of Judy Reade, librarian, Miriam Walls, Information Management Specialist, Mark Hubley, 78th Schoolmaster, who conducted a tour of the Citadel, which formed the basis for the tour described in the book and Pipe-Major Fraser Clark. Andrew Phillips, Interpretation Programs Co-ordinator for the Citadel, kindly read and commented on the manuscript before publication and assisted with many details.

The Halifax Citadel Regimental Association is an integral partner in the activities at the Citadel. As tour guide for numerous groups visiting Halifax, I wish to thank the association for their contribution to making Citadel a major attraction. It is pleasure to dedicate this book to the Halifax Citadel Regimental Association.

Brian Cuthbertson
April, 2001

Illustration Sources

NSARM — Nova Scotia Archives and Records Management; PCHDC — Parks Canada Halifax Defence Complex

Chapter 2. p.22, Wellington Museum; p.26 (T), NSARM; p.26 (B) PCHDC; p.31, NSARM; p.32, Dalhousie University Archives Oland Coll.; p.33, *Dominion Illustrated*; p.36, Dalhousie University Archives; p. 37, *Picturesque Canada*; p. 38, NSARM 1979-147.85; p.39 (T) *Dominion Illustrated*; p. 39 (B) NSARM; pp.40-41, *Dominion Illustrated*; p.42, PCHDC; p.43, Dalhousie University Killam Library. W. Morse Coll.; p.45, Queen's Own Highland Regiment; p. 47, *Dominion Illustrated* 21 Feb. 1891, Special Collections Killam Library Dalhousie University; p.48, *Dominion Illustrated*; p.50, PCHDC; p.51, NSARM 1979-147-343; p. 52, PCHDC; p.53, Government House; p.54(T), NSARM Portrait #8315; p.54(B) NSARM; p.55, PCHDC; p.56 PCHDC; Nova Scotia Museum by A. Vienneau; p.58, NSARM; p.59, *Picturesque Canada*; p.60, PCHDC; p.61 PCHDC by David B. Gillespie; p.62, NSARM; pp.66 & 67 Brian Cuthbertson; p.70 NSARM.

For information on the Halifax Citadel Regimental Association visit www.regimental.com

Index